LEITH'S
EASY
DINNER PARTIES

LEITH'S
EASY
DINNER PARTIES

Caroline Waldegrave, Puff Fairclough and Janey Orr

Photographs by Graham Kirk

BLOOMSBURY

First published in Great Britain 1995
Bloomsbury Publishing Plc, 38 Soho Square
London W1V 5DF

This edition first published in Great Britain in 1999

Copyright © 1995 and 1999 by Leith's School of Food and Wine Ltd

The moral right of the authors has been asserted

A CIP record for this book
is available from the British Library

ISBN 0 7475 4658 4

10 9 8 7 6 5 4 3 2 1

Typeset by Hewer Text Composition Services, Edinburgh
Printed in Great Britain by The Bath Press

Photographer: Graham Kirk
Stylist: Helen Payne
Home economists: Puff Fairclough and Janey Orr
Illustration by: Kate Simunek

LEITH'S

The matching of good wine with good food adds to the pleasure of each and that is why Leith's is delighted to continue its long association with one of the world's greatest family wine companies, Baron Philippe de Rothschild.

Best known for its outstanding portfolio of vintage Bordeaux wines including the Mouton Cadet range, the recently introduced Cadet Claret, and of course, the renowned Château Mouton Rothschild; it is now also producing popular varietals from the Languedoc-Roussillon, one of France's oldest wine producing regions.

We hope you enjoy the recipes in this *Easy Dinner Parties* book, many of which are ideal partners for a wine from Baron Philippe de Rothschild.

Caroline Waldegrave

THE WINES OF
BARON PHILIPPE DE ROTHSCHILD
L'ART DE L'ASSEMBLAGE

The winemakers at Baron Philippe de Rothschild are experts in the art of 'assemblage' – selecting and combining different cuvées (parcels of wine) to produce a wine that is greater than the sum of its parts.

This famous family-owned company is now run by Baroness Philippine de Rothschild, the founder's daughter. Not only is she the owner of three great Pauillac Châteaux – Clerc Milon, d'Armailhac and the incomparable Mouton Rothschild – but the company is also the largest exporter of vintage Bordeaux Appellation Contrôlée wines.

Mouton Cadet Rouge, the world's best known Bordeaux wine, combines Cabernet Sauvignon, Cabernet Franc and Merlot grapes in a vintage wine of balance, roundness and consistent quality. Mouton Cadet Blanc is an elegant dry white wine made from Semillon, Sauvignon Blanc and Muscadelle grapes. Cadet Claret is a classic Bordeaux red wine, which is fruity and soft and ready for immediate drinking.

The company's winemakers recently turned their skills of 'assemblage' to making quality wine from grapes grown outside the Bordeaux region, and the result is four single varietal wines from the Languedoc-Roussillon, one of France's oldest wine-producing areas. This vintage range includes Cabernet Sauvignon, Merlot, Chardonnay and Sauvignon Blanc.

There are many other wines within the Baron Philippe de Rothschild portfolio including the Heritage Collection, a special selection of five wines from the great Appellations of Bordeaux bearing the names of Baroness Philippine de Rothschild's ancestors; and a range of eight wines from the classic Bordeaux regions.

CONTENTS

ACKNOWLEDGEMENTS

Writing this book has been just like trying to create the perfect dinner party and we have been fortunate that many friends and colleagues have given their help and advice so freely.

As usual, all the recipes have come under the close scrutiny of the staff at Leith's, and there is no better critic than a cookery teacher! Thanks to them all for their contributions, particularly to Jacqui Thomas for her recipe ideas, Eithne Swann for managing the recipe testing so marvellously, and to Gaynor Cauter for her help with the manuscript at every stage.

We were thrilled that Juliet Harbutt agreed to write the cheese chapter and special thanks go to her for her inspiration and expertise.

Many thanks to *House & Garden* for permitting us to use recipes first published in their magazine.

Graham Kirk took the mouthwatering photographs which were so creatively styled by Helen Payne. In the studio David Barratt and Terry Ferris gave us expert, willing and cheerful help.

Our heartfelt thanks go to everyone involved at Bloomsbury, particularly Monica Macdonald and David Reynolds.

Finally, we would like to thank, with much love, Andrew, Tony and Puff's mother, for all their help and encouragement.

FOREWORD

This book has been a joy to work on. It is the book I've always wanted to have in my kitchen.

There are, of course, occasions when you can spend two days planning, shopping, organizing and cooking for a dinner party. These, however, are few and very far between. Most of us rush home from work, have a desultory tidy-up and try to lay the table as the telephone rings, the children have difficulty with their homework, the cat brings in a mouse, the bathwater runs cold and the door-to-door salesman tries to sell yet more dusters. In spite of all that, with this book, elegant yet simple dinner parties are possible. We have included in it many convenience foods that we are not ashamed to have in our supermarket trolley.

I do hope that you enjoy cooking from this book. I have so enjoyed working with Puff and Janey who are the originators of most of these recipes.

CAROLINE WALDEGRAVE
Principal, Leith's School of Food and Wine

INTRODUCTION

This book is something of a departure for Leith's. We are not aiming to teach new skills, although we hope that you will pick some up along the way. It is for everyone who loves to entertain but doesn't always have hours to prepare. We use shortcuts and convenience foods if they are appropriate and don't compromise the end result.

We have written *Leith's Easy Dinner Parties* for the cook who arrives home at 6.30 with guests arriving at 8.30, and who also wants a relaxing bath and a drink! All the recipes are written for six people, but are easily adapted (see Catering Quantities, page xvii). This is dinner-party food, but none of the recipes are complex. You may not flabbergast your guests with your skills and techniques, but the evening will be memorable, with a calm and relaxed cook sitting at the table, not stuck behind the kitchen door.

Some of the recipes have a long list of ingredients, but they are not complicated because of this, in fact they are often the easiest. We have included plenty of fish and pasta dishes, not just for their general popularity, but because both these foods cook especially quickly. In our meat and poultry dishes we have used quick-cooking cuts of meat and portions of poultry rather than whole joints or birds.

Some of the dishes are inexpensive and some are more extravagant. Most of the ingredients are easily available in urban and rural supermarkets alike. With the wide range of herbs now available, we always use fresh. Good mail order suppliers are another great source of top-quality ingredients and we have included a list of some of our favourites at the back of the book.

How the Book Works

We have written *Leith's Easy Dinner Parties* as a dinner party 'handbook', always looking for ways to speed up the process. We have designed menus around each recipe, highlighted things that can be prepared in advance, and given a wine suggestion for each menu.

The Menu

From talking to the hundreds of students who come through the doors of Leith's we have discovered that menu planning is often the major hurdle to successful entertaining. Sitting for hours in front of a pile of cookbooks is simply too daunting. Yet menu planning is the most important element of a good dinner party.

A menu suggestion appears beside each recipe, with page numbers to cross-reference. These menus are easily prepared in about 90 minutes and have been designed for balance of flavour, colour and texture. There are menus to suit every time of year – for example main-course salads are perfect for the summer.

We hope that readers will enjoy devising their own menus from the recipes in this book, as well as following our suggestions, and that all the menus will prove firm favourites with dinner-party hosts and guests alike.

Preparation in Advance

Using a shaded panel, we have indicated that part of a recipe which can be prepared in advance. However, it is also possible to work straight through most of the recipes. If a marinade is called for, you will need to allow for a minimum of 30 minutes.

Instant Assembly Dishes

If time is really short, look at our instant recipes. At the beginning of the first course and pudding chapters we have listed some very fast instant assembly dishes. While these are not always original, they are delicious and often great favourites.

Accompaniment Charts

Fast dinner-party menus require delicious but very simple vegetable accompaniments – they cannot include complicated side dishes. The washed and prepared vegetables in supermarkets are a perfect shortcut if time is really limited. We have designed some easy-to-use charts on quantities, preparation and cooking to help you select the right vegetable and farinaceous dishes to go with your dinner-party menus.

Microwave Cooking

There are times when a microwave can be invaluable in speeding up the cooking process. Some recipes have been marked with the symbol *m* at the stage which could be accelerated using a microwave. As microwave ovens vary, we have not stated specific cooking times, on the assumption that you know your own oven.

Wine

Choosing wine still has an aura of mystique about it, despite the best efforts of imaginative off-licences and supermarkets. If you are in a hurry the vast choice that confronts you can be especially daunting.

We have therefore given a wine suggestion for each recipe, which we consider to be a complementary, but by no means the only, choice. Wine is ultimately a matter of very personal taste, so don't be afraid to drink exactly what you want!

Without wasting any more time, flick through the book, find a recipe that appeals to you, and get cooking!

CONVERSION TABLES

The tables below are approximate, and do not conform in all respects to the conventional conversions, but we have found them convenient for cooking. Use either metric or imperial measurements. But do not mix the two.

Weight

Imperial	Metric	Imperial	Metric
¼oz	7–8g	½oz	15g
¾oz	20g	1oz	30g
2oz	55g	3oz	85g
4oz (¼lb)	110g	5oz	140g
6oz	170g	7oz	200g
8oz (½lb)	225g	9oz	255g
10oz	285g	11oz	310g
12oz (¾lb)	340g	13oz	370g
14oz	400g	15oz	425g
16oz (1lb)	450g	1¼lb	560g
1½lb	675g	2lb	900g
3lb	1.35kg	4lb	1.8kg
5lb	2.3kg	6lb	2.7kg
7lb	3.2kg	8lb	3.6kg
9lb	4.0kg	10lb	4.5kg

Australian cup measures

	Metric	Imperial
1 cup flour	140g	5oz
1 cup sugar (crystal or castor)	225g	8oz
1 cup brown sugar, firmly packed	170g	6oz
1 cup icing sugar, sifted	170g	6oz
1 cup butter	225g	8oz
1 cup honey, golden syrup, treacle	370g	12oz
1 cup fresh breadcrumbs	55g	2oz
1 cup packaged dry breadcrumbs	140g	5oz
1 cup crushed biscuit crumbs	110g	4oz
1 cup rice, uncooked	200g	7oz
1 cup mixed fruit or individual fruit, such as sultanas	170g	6oz
1 cup nuts, chopped	110g	4oz
1 cup coconut, desiccated	85g	3oz

Approximate American/European conversions

Commodity	USA	Metric	Imperial
Flour	1 cup	140g	5oz
Caster and granulated sugar	1 cup	225g	8oz
Caster and granulated sugar	2 level tablespoons	30g	1oz
Brown sugar	1 cup	170g	6oz
Butter/margarine/lard	1 cup	225g	8oz
Sultanas/raisins	1 cup	200g	7oz
Currants	1 cup	140g	5oz
Ground almonds	1 cup	110g	4oz
Golden syrup	1 cup	340g	12oz
Uncooked rice	1 cup	200g	7oz
Grated cheese	1 cup	110g	4oz
Butter	1 stick	110g	4oz

Liquid measures

Imperial	ml	fl oz
1¾ pints	1000 (1 litre)	35
1 pint	570	20
¾ pint	425	15
½ pint	290	10
⅓ pint	190	6.6
¼ pint (1 gill)	150	5
4 scant tablespoons	56	2
2 scant tablespoons	28	1
1 teaspoon	5	

Australian

250ml	1 cup
20ml	1 tablespoon
5ml	1 teaspoon

Approximate American/European conversions

American	European
10 pints	4.5 litres/8 pints
2½ pints (5 cups)	1.1 litres/2 pints
1 pint/16fl oz	1 pint/20fl oz/5.75ml
1¼ cups	½ pint/10fl oz/290ml
½ cup plus 2 tablespoons	¼ pint/5fl oz/150ml
¼ cup	4 tablespoons/2fl oz/55ml
½fl oz	1 tablespoon/½fl oz/15ml
1 teaspoon	1 teaspoon/5ml

Useful measurements

Measurement	Metric	Imperial
1 American cup	225ml	8fl oz
1 egg, size 3	56ml	2fl oz
1 egg white	28ml	1fl oz
1 rounded tablespoon flour	30g	1oz
1 rounded tablespoon cornflour	30g	1oz
1 rounded tablespoon caster sugar	30g	1oz
2 rounded tablespoons fresh breadcrumbs	30g	1oz
2 level teaspoons gelatine	8g	¼oz

30g/1oz granular (packet) aspic sets 570ml (1 pint) liquid.

15g/½oz powdered gelatine, or 4 leaves, will set 570ml (1 pint) liquid. (However, in hot weather, or if the liquid is very acid, like lemon juice, or if the jelly contains solid pieces of food and is to be turned out of the dish or mould, 20g/¾oz should be used.)

Wine quantities

Imperial	ml	fl oz
Average wine bottle	750	25
1 glass wine	100	3½
1 glass port or sherry	70	2
1 glass liqueur	45	1

Lengths

Imperial	Metric
½in	1cm
1in	2.5cm
2in	5cm
6in	15cm
12in	30cm

Oven temperatures

°C	°F	Gas mark	AMERICAN	AUSTRALIAN
70	150	¼	COOL	VERY SLOW
80	175	¼	COOL	VERY SLOW
100	200	½	COOL	VERY SLOW
110	225	½	COOL	VERY SLOW
130	250	1	VERY SLOW	VERY SLOW
140	275	1	VERY SLOW	SLOW
150	300	2	SLOW	SLOW
170	325	3	MODERATE	MODERATELY SLOW
180	350	4	MODERATE	MODERATELY SLOW
190	375	5	MODERATELY HOT	MODERATE
200	400	6	FAIRLY HOT	MODERATE
220	425	7	HOT	MODERATELY HOT
230	450	8	VERY HOT	MODERATELY HOT
240	475	8	VERY HOT	HOT
250	500	9	EXTREMELY HOT	HOT
270	525	9	EXTREMELY HOT	VERY HOT
290	550	9	EXTREMELY HOT	VERY HOT

MENU PLANNING

The most obvious rule, but the most important, must be to **keep it simple**. There is no point in attempting so much that the quality of execution is threatened. This is particularly important with speedy cookery. Don't try to be too clever.

Don't be too proud to stick the plan of action on the wall and follow it slavishly. Professional cooks do it all the time and it saves their sanity. It also saves a lot of time.

Balance is all: It is possible to have a seven-course meal of such exquisite balance that the guests go home at midnight feeling fit for a day's work, and equally to produce two courses so out of kilter as to make everyone feel bloated and ill, and fit for nothing.

The commonest problem is simply too much rich food. The French, great cooks and great gastronomes that they are, are heavily to blame. The secret is not to abandon creamy or buttery dishes, but to limit their size and number.

The main things to aim for are plenty of fresh vegetables and fruit, some starch, and not too many fatty foods or meaty ones.

Menu content: There are also a few mental checks that you should run through when planning a menu, as much for the gastronomic pleasure and interest of the diner as for healthy eating.

1. Avoid too many eggs in the meal.
2. Check that the vegetables are sufficiently interesting. Avoid two members of the same family (e.g. cauliflower, sprouts).
3. Check that the first or main course and the pudding are not predominantly fruit (such as melon to start, meat, poultry or fish with a fruity sauce, and fruit salad to finish).
4. Check that ingredients are not repeated.
5. Check that no two courses contain similar poultry or meat, e.g. chicken liver pâté, coq au vin.
6. Check that the meal contains good colour, texture and taste contrast.
7. Check that the wines are in the right order and are suitable to accompany the food. In brief: red should follow white, older wines should follow younger ones; strong big wines should follow delicate light ones; white wines go with fish, white meat and delicate poultry; red wines go with red meat, poultry, game and cheese.

Colour: Unless you are deliberately designing a dish or a menu to suit a colour theme, such as an all-red fruit salad, the best rule is contrast without garishness. The commonest problem is too white a meal – pale soup, chicken, cauliflower, rice, meringues and cream.

Texture: Again, contrast is the thing. If the main course is a tender casserole served with mashed potatoes to mop up the gravy, provide something crunchy, such as crisp French beans, to go with it. Some cooks have found their food processors too seductive to resist and the result can be a smooth pâté, followed by lasagne, followed by floating islands, so that guests long for something they can quite literally get their teeth into.

CATERING QUANTITIES

When catering for more than 6 people it is useful to know how much food to allow per person. As a general rule, the more people you are catering for the less food per head you need to provide, e.g. 255g/8oz stewing beef per head is essential for 4 people, but 170g/6oz per head would feed 60 people.

SOUP
Allow 290ml/½ pint soup per person.

POULTRY
Chicken and turkey Allow 450g/1lb per person, weighed when plucked and drawn. An average chicken serves 4 people on the bone and 6 people off the bone. Allow 200g/7oz raw breast off the bone per person.

Duck A 3kg/6lb bird will feed 3–4 people; a 2kg/4lb bird will feed 2 people. 1 duck makes enough pâté for 6 people.

Goose Allow 3.4kg/8lb for 4 people; 6.9kg/15lb for 7 people.

GAME
Pheasant Allow 1 bird for 2 people (roast); 1 bird for 3 people (casseroled).

Pigeon Allow 1 bird per person

Grouse Allow 1 young grouse per person (roast); 2 birds for 3 people (casseroled).

Quail Allow 2 small birds per person or 1 large boned stuffed bird served on a croûton.

Partridge Allow 1 bird per person.

Venison Allow 170g/6oz lean meat per person; 2kg/4lb cut of haunch weighed on the bone for 8–9 people.

Steaks Allow 170g/6oz per person.

MEAT
LAMB OR MUTTON
Casseroled 285g/10oz per person (boneless, with fat trimmed away).

Roast leg 1.35kg/3lb for 3–4 people; 2kg/4lb for 4–5 people; 3kg/6lb for 7–8 people.

Roast shoulder 2kg/4lb shoulder for 5–6 people; 3kg/6lb shoulder for 7–9 people.

Roast breast 450g/1lb for 2 people.

Grilled best end cutlets 3–4 per person.
Grilled loin chops 2 per person.

BEEF
Stewed 225g/8oz boneless trimmed meat per person.

Roast (off the bone) If serving men only, 225g/8oz per person; if serving men and women, 200g/7oz per person.

Roast (on the bone) 340g/12oz per person.

Roast whole fillet 2kg/4lb piece for 10 people.

Grilled steaks 200–225g/7–8oz per person depending on appetite.

PORK
Casseroled 170g/6oz per person.

Roast leg or loin (off the bone) 200g/7oz per person.

Roast leg or loin (on the bone) 340g/12oz per person.

2 average fillets will feed 3–4 people.

Grilled 1 × 170g/6oz chop or cutlet per person.

VEAL
Stews or pies 225g/8oz pie veal per person.
Fried 1 × 170g/6oz escalope per person.

FISH
Whole large fish (e.g. sea bass, salmon, whole haddock), weighed, uncleaned, with head on: 340–450g/12oz–1lb per person.

Cutlets and steaks 170g/6oz per person.

Fillets (e.g. sole, lemon sole, plaice): 3 small fillets per person (total weight about 170g/6oz).

Whole small fish (e.g. trout, slip soles, small plaice, small mackerel, herring) 225–340g/8–12oz weighed with heads for main course; 170g/6oz for first course.

Fish off the bone (in fish pie, with sauce, etc.)
170g/6oz per person.

SHELLFISH
Prawns 55–85g/2–3oz per person as a first
course; 140g/5oz per person as a main course.
Mixed shellfish 55–85g/2–3oz per person as a
first course; 140g/5oz per person as a main
course.

VEGETABLES
For specific information on quantities, cooking and
serving, see Vegetable Charts on pages 133–44.

PUDDINGS
Cooking apples Allow 225g/8oz a head for
puddings.
Fruit salad Allow 8 oranges, 2 apples, 2 bananas
and 450g/1lb grapes for 8 people.
Mousses Allow 290ml/½ pint double cream
inside and 290ml/½ pint to decorate a mousse for
8 people.
Strawberries Allow 110g/4oz a head.

CANAPÉS
Allow 4–5 canapés per person with pre-dinner
drinks.

FOOD PRESENTATION

If food looks delicious, people are predisposed to think that it tastes delicious. Food can often be particularly attractively presented on individual plates, and many of the recipes in this book specify individual servings rather than from one big dish. Serving at the table can be rather fraught, and there is also the risk of the food getting cold by the time everyone is served. So it is often preferable to present individual servings which can be arranged in the kitchen and brought straight to the table.

At Leith's School we have gradually developed a set of rules which can be used as guidelines when presenting food. Fashion may dictate the method – be it stylish *nouvelle cuisine* or chunky real food – but the guidelines are the same.

1. Keep it warm
Always serve food on warm plates. Nothing destroys anticipation more than cold plates.

2. Keep it simple
Over-decorated food often looks messed about – no longer appetizing. The more cluttered the plate, the less attractive it inevitably becomes.

3. Keep it fresh
Nothing looks more off-putting than tired food. Salad wilts when dressed in advance; sautéed potatoes become dull and dry when kept warm for hours, and whipped cream goes buttery in a warm room, so don't risk it.

4. Keep it relevant
A sprig of fresh watercress complements lamb cutlets nicely. The texture, taste and colour all do something for the lamb. But scratchy sprigs of parsley, though they might provide the colour, are unpleasant to eat.

5. Best side uppermost
Usually the side of a steak or a cutlet that is grilled or fried first looks the best, and should be placed uppermost. Bones are generally unsightly and, if they cannot be clipped off or removed, should be tucked out of the way.

6. Centre height
Dishes served on platters, such as chicken sauté, meringues, profiteroles or even a bean salad, are best given 'centre height' – arranged so that the mound of food is higher in the middle with sides sloping down. Coat carefully and evenly with the sauce, if any. Do not overload serving platters with food, which makes dishing up difficult.

7. A generous look
Tiny piped cream stars, or sparsely dotted nuts, or mean-looking chocolate curls on a mousse look amateurish and stingy.

8. Avoid clumsiness
On the other hand, the temptation to cram the last spoonful of rice into the bowl, or squeeze the last slice of pâté on to the dish, leads to a clumsy look, and can be daunting to the diner.

9. Overlapping
Chops, steaks, sliced meats, even rashers of bacon, look best evenly overlapping. This way, more of them can be fitted comfortably on the serving dish than if placed side by side.

10. Contrasting rows
Biscuits, petits fours, little cakes and cocktail canapés all look good if arranged in rows, each row consisting of one variety, rather than dotted about. Pay attention to contrasting colour, taking care, say, not to put two rows of chocolate biscuits side by side, or two rows of white sandwiches.

11. Diagonal lines
Diamond shapes and diagonal lines are easier to achieve than straight ones. The eye is more conscious of unevenness in verticals, horizontals and rectangles.

12. Not too many colours
As with any design, it is easier to get a pleasing effect if the colours are controlled – say, just green and white, or just pink and green, or chocolate and coffee colours or even two shades of one colour. Adding every available garnish to a salad tends to look garish. There are exceptions,

of course: a colourful salad Niçoise can be as pleasing to the eye as a dish of candy-coated chocolate drops.

13. Contrasting the simple and the elaborate

If the dish or bowl is elaborately decorated, contrastingly simple food tends to show it off better. A Victorian fruit épergne with ornate stem and silver carving will look stunning filled with fresh strawberries. Conversely, a plain white plate sets off pretty food design to perfection.

14. Uneven numbers

As a rule, uneven numbers of, say, rosettes of cream on a sweet soufflé or portions of meat on a platter look better than even numbers. This is especially true of small numbers.

FOOD SAFETY

These are the most important factors to take into account for food safety.

1. Bugs like warmth, moisture and to be left undisturbed, so try not to give them these ideal conditions.
2. Keep cooking utensils and hands clean. Change J-cloths, tea towels and washing-up brushes regularly.
3. Store raw meat at the bottom of the refrigerator, so that any meat juices cannot drip on to cooked food.
4. Wrap food up loosely, let it breathe.
5. Don't put hot food into the refrigerator – it will raise the temperature. Refrigerators should be kept at 5°C.
6. Get food to cool down as quickly as possible.
7. Never cover cooling hot food.
8. Avoid cross-contamination of germs – store raw and cooked foods separately as far as possible. If you mix raw and cooked foods they should both be cold and then reheated thoroughly. Avoid keeping food warm for any length of time: it should be either hot or cold.
9. Never cook large items (e.g. whole chickens) from frozen.
10. Salmonella in eggs: consumption of raw eggs or uncooked dishes made from them, such as home-made mayonnaise, mousse and ice cream, carries the risk of food poisoning. If you do use raw eggs, make sure that you use only the freshest (pasteurized eggs are available), that the dishes are eaten as soon as possible after making and that they are never left for more than 1 hour at room temperature.

Vulnerable people such as the elderly, the sick, babies, toddlers and pregnant women should only eat eggs that have been thoroughly cooked until both white and yolk are solid.

FIRST COURSES

INSTANT FIRST COURSES

With French or Italian Bread

Make bruschetta with baguette or ciabatta:
slice thickly on the diagonal, brush with olive oil
and garlic and toast lightly on each side. Top with:

- Pesto; rocket paste; artichoke paste; green or
  black olive tapenade or truffle paste.
- Sliced mozzarella; crumbled feta; thinly shaved
  Parmesan or Pecorino cheese; fromage blanc or
  Roquefort. Garnish with fresh herbs, chopped
  olives or black pepper.
- Slices of fresh plum tomatoes or slivers of sun-
  dried tomatoes and pomodoro sauce.
- Chopped tomato, avocado, black olives and
  basil with Greek yoghurt.
- Spanish onion, thinly sliced and sweated in
  olive oil until soft and caramelized, garnished
  with chopped thyme.
- Field mushrooms sweated in butter with garlic
  until soft, roughly chopped and garnished with
  soured cream and paprika.
- Red and yellow peppers grilled until the skins
  are black, peeled, sliced and tossed in olive oil
  and balsamic vinegar.
- Tinned tuna fish, mixed with finely chopped
  red onion, flageolet beans and olive oil,
  garnished with rocket leaves.
- Hummus garnished with chopped black olives.
- Taramasalata garnished with finely chopped
  chervil.
- Guacamole garnished with finely diced
  cucumber, red pepper and red onion.

With Rye Bread or Pumpernickel

- Gravadlax with dill mustard.
- Smoked salmon and soured cream with dill.
- Salmon roe and soured cream with chives.
- Salami and horseradish cream with parsley.
- Carpaccio with rocket and shaved Parmesan
  cheese.
- Parma ham and asparagus.
- Smoked oysters with soured cream.

Cold Meat and Fish

- Parma ham with melon; figs; thinly shaved
  Parmesan cheese; asparagus; *fruitta de
  mostarda*.
- Bresaola with thinly shaved Parmesan cheese,
  rocket and lemon juice.
- Carpaccio with soured cream and chives.
- Smoked venison with cranberry sauce or
  pickled walnuts.
- Mixed smoked platter: smoked salmon,
  smoked halibut, smoked eel, smoked trout.
  Served with brown bread, lemon and
  horseradish.
- Platters of *fruits de mer*: ask your fishmonger
  to prepare one for you.
- Caviar: 30g/1oz per person. Leave the caviar
  in its original pot. Chill and serve with
  lemon wedges, chopped hard-boiled egg
  white and sieved egg yolk (in separate
  piles), chopped parsley, chopped raw onion,
  soured cream and toast or blinis.

- Oysters: 9 or 12 per person. Ask your fishmonger to open them as late as possible or shuck them yourself if you can do this quickly and easily (see page 33). Discard the top shells and check the bottom shells for any bits of shell or grit but leave any sea water or juice. Serve with Tabasco sauce or chilli pepper, freshly ground black pepper, lemon wedges, vinegar and brown bread and butter.
- Brown shrimps: 150ml/¼ pint per person. Serve peeled with hot bread, good butter, lemon wedges and salt and freshly ground black pepper. Provide finger-bowls.

Eggs

- Scrambled eggs (1–2 per person) flavoured with anchovy paste, smoked salmon, chopped mushrooms, sorrel, chervil or slivers of truffle.
- Poached quail's eggs (2 per person) with spinach salad and bacon, or steamed asparagus, on puff pastry with Hollandaise.

Fruit and Vegetables

- Mixed griddled vegetables: aubergines, courgettes, peppers, mushrooms, red onions, artichoke hearts, asparagus.
- Asparagus with butter, olive oil, French dressing or Hollandaise.
- Avocado with French dressing, Greek yoghurt or pesto.
- Ripe pears peeled and thinly sliced, served with Stilton, Roquefort, Parmesan or Cambozola cheese.
- Grilled radicchio with French dressing and artichoke hearts.
- Galia, honeydew and watermelon balled and tossed with chopped mint leaves.
- Aubergine, cut into large chunks and griddled or fried, tossed in olive oil and served with pesto and Parmesan or feta cheese, or mustardy French dressing, or tahini and toasted sesame seeds, or chopped dill and lemon juice, or green olives, chopped thyme and lemon juice.
- Ripe beef tomatoes with grilled halloumi cheese, olive oil and basil.

SOUPS
Almond and Parsley Soup

SERVES 6

45g/1½oz butter

1 Spanish onion, finely chopped

1 large potato, peeled and finely chopped

860ml/1½ pints chicken or vegetable stock (see
  pages 185, 186) or water

290ml/½ pint milk

salt and freshly ground black pepper

140g/5oz ground almonds

4 tablespoons finely chopped parsley

150ml/5fl oz crème fraîche

1. Preheat the oven to 200°C/400°F/gas mark 6.

2. Melt the butter in a large saucepan, add the onion and potato and sweat until the onion is soft but not coloured. Add the stock or water and the milk and season lightly with salt and pepper. Bring to the boil, then reduce the heat and simmer gently until the potato is cooked.

3. Liquidize the soup and push through a sieve into the rinsed-out pan.

4. Meanwhile, sprinkle the ground almonds on a baking sheet and toast in the oven until golden-brown. Add to the pan with the parsley and liquidize the soup, in batches if necessary, until smooth.

5. Season to taste with salt and pepper, add the crème fraîche and reheat gently without boiling.

6. To serve: pour into 6 individual soup bowls.

PALO CORTADO SHERRY

ALMOND AND PARSLEY SOUP

HALIBUT WITH CARAMELIZED
CHICORY
(see page 68)

MANGO, RASPBERRY AND
BLUEBERRY CLAFOUTIS
(see page 149)

Carrot and Cumin Soup

SERVES 6

30g/1oz butter

1 large onion, finely chopped

2 cloves of garlic, unpeeled

2 teaspoons ground cumin

900g/2lb carrots, peeled and grated

1 litre/1¾ pints chicken or vegetable stock (see
  pages 185,186)

salt and freshly ground black pepper

TO GARNISH

2 tablespoons snipped chives

1. Melt the butter in a large saucepan, add the onion and sweat until soft but not coloured.

2. Blanch the garlic in a small pan of boiling water for 3 minutes, then refresh under running cold water. Peel and crush the garlic and add to the onion with the cumin. Increase the heat and cook, stirring constantly, until the onion is lightly browned. Add the carrots and stock and season to taste with salt and pepper. Bring to the boil, then reduce the heat and simmer for 5 minutes.

3. Liquidize the soup, in batches if necessary.

4. To serve: reheat. Pour into 6 individual soup bowls and sprinkle with the chives.

NOTE: This soup is equally delicious served cold.

MANZANILLA SHERRY

↜

CARROT AND CUMIN SOUP

GRILLED CURED SALMON SALAD
WITH HORSERADISH DRESSING
(see page 104)

PRUNE AND CHOCOLATE
PUDDINGS
(see page 167)

↜

Cucumber and Melon Gazpacho

SERVES 6

2 large cucumbers, peeled and deseeded

1 medium Galia melon, peeled and deseeded

1 bunch of rocket leaves

3 sprigs of dill

3 sprigs of mint

2 tablespoons tarragon vinegar

1 small clove of garlic, peeled

1 small green chilli, deseeded

290ml/½ pint carrot juice or mixed vegetable juice

150ml/5fl oz Greek yoghurt

6 tablespoons olive oil

salt and freshly ground black pepper

TO GARNISH

ice, crushed

sprigs of dill

1. Finely dice half 1 cucumber and 1 slice of melon and reserve.

2. Chop the remaining cucumber and melon roughly and put into a liquidizer with the rocket, dill, mint, vinegar, garlic, chilli and half the carrot or mixed vegetable juice. Liquidize to a smooth paste and gradually blend in the remaining juice, yoghurt and oil. Season to taste with salt and pepper. Refrigerate until cold.

3. To serve: pour into 6 individual soup bowls and garnish with the reserved cucumber and melon, crushed ice cubes and sprigs of dill.

FINO SHERRY

CUCUMBER AND MELON
GAZPACHO

LAMB CUTLETS WITH SUN-DRIED
TOMATO AND CHILLI COUSCOUS
(see page 93)

CHOCOLATE BREAD AND
BUTTER PUDDING
(see page 153)

Roast Sweet Pepper Soup

SERVES 6

6 red peppers

3 yellow peppers

2 cloves of garlic, unpeeled

1 litre/1¾ pints chicken stock (see page 185) or
   water

½ tablespoon balsamic vinegar

salt and freshly ground black pepper

TO GARNISH

110g/4oz feta cheese, crumbled

1 tablespoon finely chopped thyme

1. Preheat the oven to 200°C/400°F/gas mark 6.

2. Put the peppers and garlic on to a baking sheet and roast in the oven for about 15 minutes, turning once, until they are soft and the skins shrivelled and black. Allow to cool completely in a paper or plastic bag.

3. When the peppers are cold, peel off the skins and remove the stalks, membrane and seeds. Peel the garlic and put into a food processor with the peppers and their juice and half the stock or water. Process to a smooth purée and pour into a large saucepan. Add the vinegar and the remaining stock or water. Season to taste with salt and pepper and reheat gently without boiling.

4. To serve: pour into 6 individual soup bowls and sprinkle with the feta cheese and thyme.

ROSÉ DE PROVENCE

ROAST SWEET PEPPER SOUP

CHICKEN SAUTÉ WITH GREEN
OLIVES
(see page 74)

APPLES WITH CARAMELIZED
CRESCENTS
(see page 160)

Sweet Potato and Mushroom Soup

SERVES 6

30g/1oz butter

1 onion, finely chopped

*2 medium pink-skinned sweet potatoes, peeled and
chopped*

1 clove of garlic, thinly sliced

1 sprig of thyme

*30g/1oz dried wild mushrooms, soaked in 150ml/
5fl oz hot water*

450g/1lb field mushrooms, chopped

3 tablespoons Madeira

*870ml/1½ pints chicken stock (see page 185) or
water*

salt and freshly ground black pepper

150ml/5fl oz double cream

freshly grated nutmeg

SWEET POTATO AND
MUSHROOM SOUP

HALIBUT STEAKS WITH CASHEW
NUTS AND CHEESE
(see page 67)

PASSIONFRUIT AND MUSCAT
SYLLABUB
(see page 169)

---

1. Melt the butter in a large saucepan, add the onion and sweat until soft but not coloured. Add the sweet potatoes, garlic and thyme and cook over a low heat for 5 further minutes.

2. Strain the soaked wild mushrooms through absorbent paper, reserving the soaking liquid. Add the soaked mushrooms to the pan with the field mushrooms.

3. Cook for 5 further minutes until the mushrooms are soft, then add the Madeira. Bring to the boil, then reduce the heat and simmer for 2–3 minutes.

4. Add the stock and mushroom liquid and season lightly with salt and pepper. Bring to the boil, then reduce the heat and simmer for 10 minutes.

5. Liquidize the soup until smooth.

6. Return to the rinsed-out pan, add the cream and season to taste with nutmeg and salt and pepper. Reheat gently without boiling.

7. To serve: pour into 6 individual soup bowls.

PALO CORTADO SHERRY

Prawn and Watercress Soup

SERVES 6

1.35kg/3lb cooked in-shell prawns

1 litre/1¾ pints water

juice of 1 lemon

55g/2oz butter

1 large onion, finely chopped

2 bunches of watercress, chopped

salt and freshly ground black pepper

1. Peel the prawns and put the shells into a saucepan with the water and lemon juice. Bring to the boil, then reduce the heat and simmer for 15 minutes.

2. Meanwhile, melt the butter in a frying pan, add the onion and sweat until soft but not coloured.

3. Strain the prawn shell stock and process with the onion and prawns until smooth, in batches if necessary.

4. Put into a saucepan and stir in the watercress. Season to taste with salt and pepper and reheat briefly, taking care not to allow the soup to boil or the watercress will discolour and prawns toughen.

5. To serve: pour into 6 individual soup bowls.

NEW ZEALAND SAUVIGNON BLANC

PRAWN AND WATERCRESS SOUP

RACK OF LAMB WITH MUSTARD
AND BREADCRUMBS
(see page 96)

A SELECTION OF CHEESES
(see page 176)

Mussel and Saffron Broth

Farmed mussels, now widely available, are much easier and less time-consuming to clean than wild ones.

SERVES 6

900g/2lb mussels

570ml/1 pint dry white wine

290ml/½ pint water

1 large onion, finely chopped

3 cloves of garlic, bruised

2 tablespoons chopped parsley

15g/½oz butter

6 shallots, finely chopped

2 large pinches of saffron strands

675g/1½lb ripe beef tomatoes, peeled, deseeded and finely chopped

salt and freshly ground black pepper

1 bunch of dill

1. Clean the mussels by scrubbing them well under running cold water. Pull away the beards and discard any mussels that are cracked or that remain open when tapped.

2. Put the wine, water, onion, garlic and parsley into a large saucepan. Bring to the boil, then reduce the heat and simmer for 15 minutes.

3. Add the mussels, cover and cook over a low heat for about 5 minutes until the shells open, shaking the pan occasionally.

4. Drain the mussels through a double thickness of muslin or cheesecloth, reserving the cooking liquid. Discard any mussels that have not opened.

5. When the mussels are cool enough to handle, remove the meat and set aside. Discard the shells.

6. Melt the butter in a large saucepan, add the shallots and sweat until soft but not coloured. Infuse the saffron in 2 tablespoons boiling water and add to the shallots with the strained mussel cooking liquid and the tomatoes. Season to taste with salt and pepper and simmer for 5 minutes. Add the mussels and dill and reheat briefly without boiling.

7. To serve: pour into 6 individual soup bowls.

NOTE: If no muslin or cheesecloth is available use a very clean tea towel.

MUSCADET DE SÈVRE-ET-MAINE SUR LIE

MUSSEL AND SAFFRON BROTH

LEMON CHICKEN WITH CREAM CHEESE AND HERBS
(see page 76)

RUBY RED FRUIT PARCELS
(see page 158)

Prosciutto and Cannellini Bean Soup

SERVES 6

30g/1oz butter

1 large onion, finely chopped

85g/3oz prosciutto, roughly chopped

1 × 400g/14oz tin of cannellini beans, drained

1 litre/1¾ pints chicken stock (see page 185)

2 tablespoons finely chopped sage

salt and freshly ground black pepper

TO SERVE

12 garlic and herb croûtons (see page 13)

1. Melt the butter in a large saucepan, add the onion and sweat until soft but not coloured. Add the prosciutto and cook with the onions until crisp.

2. Purée the cannellini beans in a liquidizer or food processor and add to the pan with the stock and sage.

3. Season to taste with salt and pepper and simmer for 10 minutes.

4. To serve: pour into 6 individual soup bowls and hand the garlic and herb croûtons separately.

CHILLED BEAUJOLAIS

PROSCIUTTO AND CANNELLINI
BEAN SOUP

PORK MEDALLIONS WITH
YELLOW PEPPER RELISH
(see page 100)

MACERATED STRAWBERRIES
(see page 165)

Garlic and Herb Croûtons

SERVES 6

1 small baguette, cut into 5mm/¼in slices

2 cloves of garlic, crushed

1 tablespoon finely chopped parsley

½ teaspoon finely chopped sage

30g/1oz butter, softened

1. Preheat the grill to its highest setting.

2. Toast the baguette slices lightly on one side.

3. Mix the garlic, parsley, sage and butter to a paste and spread over the untoasted sides of the baguette slices.

4. Toast until the butter has melted and browned lightly. Cut each slice into 2 on the diagonal and serve.

FIRST-COURSE SALADS
Couscous Salad with Grilled Aubergines

SERVES 6

225g/8oz precooked couscous (see note)

8 dried apricots, chopped

290ml/½ pint carrot juice or mixed vegetable juice

150ml/5fl oz orange juice

2 tablespoons red wine vinegar

1 medium aubergine

½ tablespoon chilli oil

2 tablespoons olive oil

salt and freshly ground black pepper

3 strips of orange zest

1 bunch of chives, chopped

2 tablespoons pinenuts, toasted

**COUSCOUS SALAD WITH
GRILLED AUBERGINES**

VEAL MARTINI
(see page 92)

LEMON SYLLABUB
(see page 170)

1. Put the couscous and apricots into a large bowl. Put the carrot or mixed vegetable juice, orange juice and vinegar into a saucepan, bring to the boil and pour over the couscous. Leave to stand for 15 minutes.

2. Meanwhile, preheat the grill to its highest setting. Cut the aubergine into 6 × 1cm/½in slices on the diagonal. Mix the chilli and olive oils and brush over both sides of the aubergine slices. Season with salt and pepper and grill on both sides until the aubergine is dark golden-brown and soft.

3. Cut the orange zest into thin julienne strips and blanch in a small pan of boiling water for 30 seconds. Drain and refresh under running cold water.

4. Fluff up the couscous with a fork and mix in the chives and pinenuts. Season to taste with salt and pepper.

5. To serve: put a slice of aubergine on to each of 6 individual serving plates and pile the couscous salad on top. Garnish with the orange julienne.

NOTE: Most couscous sold in this country is precooked and only requires soaking.

SAINT-VÉRAN

Warm Puy Lentil Salad

SERVES 6

225g/8oz Puy lentils (see note)

1 small onion, halved

1 strip of orange zest

2 bay leaves

110g/4oz piece of pancetta or rindless streaky
   bacon

1 tablespoon walnut oil

2 small red onions, finely chopped

1 yellow pepper, deseeded and diced

salt and freshly ground black pepper

1 orange, peeled, pith removed and segmented

6 spring onions, sliced on the diagonal

FOR THE VINAIGRETTE

6 tablespoons olive oil

2 tablespoons walnut oil

2 tablespoons cider vinegar

2 tablespoons orange juice

WARM PUY LENTIL SALAD

**CRUSTED COD STEAKS WITH
ROCKET PASTE**

(see page 64)

**CHOCOLATE RUM AND
RAISIN PUDDINGS**

(see page 154)

2.5cm/1in piece of fresh root ginger, peeled and
   grated

salt and freshly ground black pepper

TO SERVE

oakleaf lettuce and radicchio leaves

1. Wash the lentils and pick them over carefully. Put them into a large saucepan with the onion, orange zest and bay leaves and enough water to cover. Bring to the boil, then reduce the heat and simmer for about 30 minutes or until the lentils are soft but still holding their shape.

2. Meanwhile, cut the pancetta or bacon into lardons 2.5cm/1in long. Heat the walnut oil in a large frying pan, add the lardons and fry until crisp. Add the onions and yellow pepper and continue to cook over a low heat until soft.

3. Drain the lentils and discard the onion, orange zest and bay leaves. Whisk together all the vinaigrette ingredients and add to the frying pan with the lentils. Bring to the boil and season to taste with salt and pepper. Add the orange segments and spring onions.

4. To serve: pile the lentil salad on to 6 individual plates and surround with the salad leaves.

NOTE: Le Puy, in the Auvergne region of central France, is famous for its tiny, dark grey-green lentils, which have a wonderful earthy flavour and retain their shape well during cooking.

FRENCH RED VIN DE PAYS

Spiced Olive and Cherry Tomato Salad

SERVES 6

225g/8oz mixed green, black and Kalamata olives,
   pitted

½ tablespoon finely chopped red chilli

2 cloves of garlic, crushed

1 red onion, finely chopped

1 tablespoon balsamic vinegar

1 tablespoon white wine vinegar

4 tablespoons extra virgin olive oil

salt and freshly ground black pepper

450g/1lb cherry tomatoes, halved

110g/4oz mozzarella cheese, cubed

2 tablespoons chopped basil

1. Put the olives, chilli, garlic and onion into a bowl. Whisk together the vinegars and oil, season to taste with salt and pepper and pour over the olives. Leave to marinate overnight.

2. To serve: add the tomatoes, mozzarella cheese and basil to the olive mixture. Mix together gently and pile on to a large serving plate.

BEAUJOLAIS

SPICED OLIVE AND CHERRY
TOMATO SALAD

SALMON BAKED WITH A SWEET
AND HOT CRUST

(see page 60)

FRIED PEARS WITH
MACADAMIAS AND PINENUTS

(see page 161)

Chicory Salad with Smoked Oysters, Pecans and Gorgonzola

SERVES 6

6 small heads of chicory

1 × 110g/4oz tin of smoked oysters, drained

110g/4oz pecan nuts

110g/4oz Gorgonzola cheese, cubed

FOR THE VINAIGRETTE

4 tablespoons olive oil

2 tablespoons hazelnut oil

2 tablespoons sherry vinegar

1 teaspoon grainy mustard

2 tablespoons crème fraîche or double cream

salt and freshly ground black pepper

1. Make the vinaigrette: put all the ingredients into a liquidizer and blend until smooth. Season to taste with salt and pepper.

2. Discard any tough outer chicory leaves and reserve 24 of the larger leaves. Chop the remaining chicory roughly.

3. Mix the chopped chicory, smoked oysters, pecan nuts and Gorgonzola cheese with the vinaigrette.

4. To serve: arrange 4 chicory leaves on each of 6 individual plates and pile the salad on top.

VOUVRAY DEMI-SEC

CHICORY SALAD WITH
SMOKED OYSTERS,
PECANS AND GORGONZOLA

FRESH HERB PASTA
(see page 120)

SUMMER RED FRUITS
MACERATED IN ELDERFLOWER
CORDIAL AND KIRSCH
(see page 164)

Bloody Mary Crab Salad

SERVES 6

900g/2lb cooked brown and white crabmeat,
*   unmixed*
½ cucumber, deseeded and diced
3 sticks of celery, diced
lemon juice
salt and freshly ground black pepper

FOR THE DRESSING

½ tablespoon Worcestershire sauce
1 tablespoon vodka
150ml/5fl oz tomato juice
¼ teaspoon Tabasco sauce
3 tablespoons mayonnaise
salt and freshly ground black pepper

TO SERVE

1 cos or romaine lettuce, torn into bite-sized pieces

1. Pick over the white and brown crabmeat, taking care to remove any small pieces of shell. Reserve the brown meat for the dressing.

2. Mix together the white crabmeat, cucumber and celery, moisten with lemon juice and season lightly with salt and pepper. Chill thoroughly.

3. Make the dressing: put all the ingredients into a liquidizer with the brown crabmeat and blend until smooth. Season to taste with salt and pepper. If the mixture is frothy, leave to stand for 10 minutes.

4. To serve: line 6 individual glass bowls or plates with lettuce leaves. Pile on the white crabmeat mixture and pour over the dressing. Serve very well chilled.

ICED VODKA

BLOODY MARY CRAB SALAD

THREE-CHEESE PASTA
(see page 124)

RUBY RED FRUIT PARCELS
(see page 158)

Prawn Salad with Pink Grapes and Cucumber

SERVES 6

450g/1lb large peeled cooked prawns

225g/8oz button mushrooms, thinly sliced

225g/8oz seedless pink grapes

½ cucumber, deseeded and cut into small dice

FOR THE MARINADE

150ml/5fl oz good-quality olive oil

1 tablespoon red wine vinegar

juice of 1 lemon

1 teaspoon Dijon mustard

½ red chilli, deseeded and finely chopped

½ teaspoon ground cumin

½ teaspoon ground coriander

½ teaspoon caster sugar

4 sprigs of chervil

TO GARNISH

1 tablespoon chopped chervil

1. Mix together all the marinade ingredients and add the prawns. Cover and leave to marinate for at least 30 minutes or overnight in the refrigerator.

2. Remove from the refrigerator at least 30 minutes before serving and add the mushrooms, grapes and cucumber.

3. To serve: pile the salad into a serving dish and sprinkle with the chervil.

AUSTRALIAN SAUVIGNON BLANC

PRAWN SALAD WITH PINK
GRAPES AND CUCUMBER

PORK MEDALLIONS WITH
BUTTER BEAN MASH
(see page 99)

PEAR AND MASCARPONE PUFFS
(see page 152)

Spinach and Bacon Salad with Red Chilli and Mango

SERVES 6

1 mango, peeled, stoned and cut into chunks

½ red chilli, deseeded and finely chopped

110g/4oz feta cheese, crumbled

5 tablespoons sunflower oil

140g/5oz piece of rindless streaky bacon, cut into
   chunks

2 thick slices of white bread, crusts removed, cut
   into cubes

salt

225g/8oz young spinach leaves, thoroughly washed

FOR THE DRESSING

6 tablespoons olive oil

2 tablespoons sherry vinegar

salt and freshly ground black pepper

1. Whisk together the dressing ingredients and season to taste with salt and pepper.

2. Mix together the mango, chilli and feta cheese.

3. Heat 1 tablespoon of the oil in a large frying pan, add the bacon and fry until crisp and golden. Remove from the pan with a slotted spoon and dry on absorbent paper.

4. Heat the remaining oil in the pan, add the bread cubes and fry until golden-brown on all sides. Remove the croûtons from the pan with a slotted spoon and drain on absorbent paper. Sprinkle lightly with salt.

5. Wipe the pan, add the bacon and the dressing and reheat briefly.

6. Put the spinach leaves and mango mixture into a large bowl. Add the bacon and hot dressing and toss thoroughly.

7. To serve: turn the salad into a serving bowl and sprinkle with the croûtons.

TAVEL ROSÉ

SPINACH AND BACON SALAD
WITH RED CHILLI AND MANGO

VENISON STEAKS WITH
CRANBERRIES AND CHESTNUTS

(see page 82)

PRUNE AND CHOCOLATE
PUDDINGS

(see page 167)

Italian Sausage, Avocado and Pesto Salad

*If you cannot find Italian sausages, use
a good-quality salami instead.*

SERVES 6

1 dried red chilli

4 tablespoons oil

1 large clove of garlic, bruised

*2 thick slices of white bread, crusts removed, cut
    into cubes*

salt

*450g/1lb Italian sausages, cut into 2.5cm/1in
    chunks*

1 cos lettuce, shredded

*2 avocado pears, peeled, stoned and cut into
    chunks*

5 tablespoons pesto sauce (see page 192)

1. Split the red chilli in half, put into a frying pan
with the oil and garlic and fry for 2 minutes.
Remove the chilli and garlic, add the bread cubes
to the flavoured oil and fry until dark golden-
brown on all sides. Remove the croûtons with a
slotted spoon and drain on absorbent paper.
Sprinkle lightly with salt.

2. Pour off the oil and wipe out the pan. Fry the
sausages for 5–6 minutes or until cooked.

3. Put the lettuce into a large bowl, add the
sausage, croûtons and avocado and pour over the
pesto sauce. Toss thoroughly.

4. To serve: transfer the salad to a serving dish.

CHILLED VALPOLICELLA

ITALIAN SAUSAGE, AVOCADO
AND PESTO SALAD

CARAMELIZED RADICCHIO PASTA
(see page 116)

LEMON AND RASPBERRY CRÈMES
(see page 156)

Warm Curried Chicken Liver Salad

SERVES 6

225g/8oz chicken livers

1 tablespoon sunflower oil

110g/4oz shiitake mushrooms, sliced

1 tablespoon red wine vinegar

4 tablespoons plain flour

3 teaspoons ground coriander

2 teaspoons ground cumin

½ teaspoon ground turmeric

½ teaspoon cayenne pepper

½ teaspoon dry English mustard

salt and freshly ground black pepper

2 tablespoons finely chopped coriander

1 head of frisée lettuce

2 tablespoons French dressing (see page 190)

1. Trim the chicken livers, taking care to remove any greenish parts as they will be bitter.

2. Heat half the oil in a large frying pan, add the mushrooms and fry for 2–3 minutes until soft. Add the vinegar and boil until the mixture is syrupy. Remove from the pan and keep warm.

3. Thoroughly combine the flour with the spices. Coat the chicken livers in the seasoned flour and pat off any excess.

4. Add the remaining oil to the pan, add the chicken livers and fry until brown on the outside but still pink in the middle. Return the mushroom mixture to the pan, season to taste with salt and pepper and stir in the chopped coriander.

5. Tear the lettuce into bite-sized pieces and toss in a large bowl with the French dressing.

6. To serve: divide the salad between 6 salad bowls or individual plates and pile the chicken liver mixture in the middle.

RED RIOJA

WARM CURRIED CHICKEN
LIVER SALAD

RED SNAPPER WITH TOMATO
AND OLIVE CONCASSE
(see page 63)

ROASTED COCONUT AND
RUM CREAM
(see page 175)

DIPS AND PÂTÉS
Roast Aubergine Dip

The following three dips can be very successfully served together with a choice of breads, Melba toast (see page 183) and vegetable crudités.

SERVES 6

3 large aubergines

1 tablespoon extra virgin olive oil

4 cloves of garlic

2 tablespoons finely chopped parsley

150ml/5fl oz Greek yoghurt

Tabasco sauce

balsamic vinegar

salt and freshly ground black pepper

55g/2oz sun-dried tomatoes in oil, drained and finely chopped

1. Preheat the oven to 190°C/375°F/gas mark 5.

2. Place the aubergines on a baking sheet, brush with the oil and roast in the oven for 40–60 minutes or until soft. Tuck the cloves of garlic, lightly oiled, under the aubergines halfway through the cooking time. Allow the aubergines to cool.

3. Peel the aubergines, put the flesh into a clean cloth and squeeze gently to extract the bitter juices. Squeeze the cloves of garlic from their skins and put into a food processor with the aubergine flesh, parsley and yoghurt. Process until smooth and season to taste with Tabasco, vinegar, salt and pepper. Stir in the sun-dried tomatoes. Chill well before serving.

TAVEL ROSÉ

ROAST AUBERGINE DIP
ROAST GARLIC DIP
OLIVE AND CHILLI DIP

SAUTÉ OF BEEF WITH
BEETROOT AND OLIVES

(see page 87)

HONEY AND FIG CUSTARDS

(see page 157)

Roast Garlic Dip

SERVES 6

1 large head of garlic, divided into cloves

1 tablespoon olive oil

150ml/5fl oz Greek yoghurt

30g/1oz walnuts, roughly chopped

1 tablespoon snipped chives

salt and freshly ground black pepper

1. Preheat the oven to 190°C/375°F/gas mark 5.

2. Place the cloves of garlic on a baking sheet and brush with the oil. Roast in the oven for 10–15 minutes or until very soft. Allow to cool.

3. Squeeze the cloves of garlic from their skins and put into a food processor with the yoghurt and walnuts. Process to a coarse paste. Stir in the chives and season to taste with salt and pepper.

NOTE: Although this seems like a large amount of garlic, roasting it gives it a very mellow flavour, not at all pungent.

TAVEL ROSÉ

ROAST AUBERGINE DIP
ROAST GARLIC DIP
OLIVE AND CHILLI DIP

SAUTÉ OF BEEF WITH
BEETROOT AND OLIVES
(see page 87)

HONEY AND FIG CUSTARDS
(see page 157)

Olive and Chilli Dip

SERVES 6

110g/4oz black olives, pitted

1 red chilli, deseeded and roughly chopped

1 tablespoon good-quality capers, drained and
  rinsed

1 clove of garlic, chopped

5 tablespoons olive oil

freshly ground black pepper

1. Put the olives, chilli, capers and garlic into a food processor and process to a paste.

2. With the motor still running, pour in the oil and process until smooth. Season to taste with pepper.

TAVEL ROSÉ

ROAST AUBERGINE DIP
ROAST GARLIC DIP
OLIVE AND CHILLI DIP

SAUTÉ OF BEEF WITH
BEETROOT AND OLIVES
(see page 87)

HONEY AND FIG CUSTARDS
(see page 157)

Three-Cheese Pâté with Pecans

SERVES 6

200g/7oz full-fat cream cheese
110g/4oz fromage frais
finely grated zest and juice of 1 lemon
salt and freshly ground white pepper
110g/4oz Dolcelatte cheese, diced
55g/2oz pecan nuts, chopped
1 tablespoon snipped chives

TO SERVE

radicchio leaves

4 tablespoons French dressing (see page 190)
12 slices of Melba toast (see page 183)

1. Line 6 ramekins with clingfilm.

2. Mix together the cream cheese, fromage frais and lemon zest and season lightly with lemon juice, salt and pepper. Divide the mixture between the ramekins, spreading it on the base and up the sides.

3. Mix the Dolcelatte cheese with the pecan nuts. Pack into the ramekins, cover and refrigerate for at least 30 minutes.

4. To serve: divide the radicchio leaves between 6 individual plates. Turn out a pâté on to each. Drizzle over the French dressing and garnish with chives. Hand the Melba toast separately.

DOLCETTO D'ALBA

THREE-CHEESE PÂTÉ
WITH PECANS

NOISETTES OF LAMB WITH
APRICOT AND CAPER JAM
(see page 98)

CHOCOLATE BREAD AND
BUTTER PUDDING
(see page 153)

Smoked Halibut Pâté

SERVES 6

225g/8oz unsalted butter, very soft
finely grated zest and juice of 2 limes
675g/1½lb smoked halibut
1 bunch of chives, chopped
freshly ground black pepper

TO SERVE

6 slices of pumpernickel bread

1. Put the butter and three-quarters of the lime zest and juice into a food processor and process until mixed. Add the smoked halibut and the chives, reserving 1 tablespoon for garnish, and process briefly to combine. Season to taste with pepper, adding the reserved lime zest and juice if necessary.

2. Line 6 ramekins with clingfilm and fill with the pâté. Smooth the tops with a knife, cover and refrigerate for at least 1 hour.

3. To serve: unmould a pâté on to each of 6 individual plates and sprinkle with the reserved chives. Hand the pumpernickel bread separately.

AUSTRALIAN CHARDONNAY

SMOKED HALIBUT PÂTÉ

FILLET STEAKS WITH PARSNIP
AND SESAME CAKES
(see page 90)

NECTARINE, STRAWBERRY AND
ALMOND SPONGE
(see page 150)

Salmon Rillettes

SERVES 6

450g/1lb poached salmon, skinned and boned
225g/8oz fromage frais
1 piece of preserved ginger, finely diced
1 tablespoon preserved ginger syrup
cayenne pepper
salt

TO SERVE

thinly sliced wholemeal bread and unsalted butter

1. Flake the salmon roughly with a fork and mix with the fromage frais, ginger and ginger syrup, taking care not to break up the salmon too much. Season to taste with cayenne pepper and salt. Chill well.

2. To serve: mound the salmon rillettes on to 6 individual plates. Hand the bread and butter separately.

MOSEL KABINETT

SALMON RILLETTES

CHICKEN LIVER AND LEMON
PASTA
(see page 131)

FIGS WITH GOAT'S CHEESE
AND PECAN CARAMEL
(see page 162)

FISH

Crab Cakes with Horseradish Relish

SERVES 6

1 × 170g/6oz tin of white crabmeat
85g/3oz butter
1 medium Spanish onion, finely chopped
340g/12oz potatoes, parboiled
1 bunch of parsley, finely chopped
salt and freshly ground black pepper
seasoned plain flour
1 tablespoon oil

FOR THE HORSERADISH RELISH

3 tablespoons grated horseradish
3 tablespoons mayonnaise
3 tablespoons Greek yoghurt
3 shallots, diced
1 Granny Smith apple, peeled and diced
salt and freshly ground black pepper

CRAB CAKES WITH
HORSERADISH RELISH

SMOKED DUCK AND
BABY CORN SALAD
(see page 110)

PASSIONFRUIT AND
MUSCAT SYLLABUB
(see page 169)

TO GARNISH

lemon wedges

1. Drain the crabmeat and flake with a fork in a bowl. Heat 30g/1oz of the butter in a saucepan until foaming, add the onion and sweat until soft but not coloured.

2. Grate the potatoes coarsely and add to the crab with the onion and the parsley. Season to taste with salt and pepper. Shape the mixture into 6 cakes and chill for 15 minutes, or overnight.

3. Meanwhile, make the horseradish relish: mix together all the ingredients and season to taste with salt and pepper. Set aside for at least 1 hour to allow the flavours to develop.

4. Coat the crab cakes with seasoned flour and pat off any excess. Heat the remaining butter and the oil in a large, heavy-bottomed frying pan until foaming. Add the crab cakes and fry over a gentle heat for at least 5 minutes until a golden-brown crust has formed on the underside. Turn the crab cakes over and fry on the other side in the same way.

5. To serve: put a crab cake on to each of 6 individual plates. Spoon a portion of horseradish relish beside each crab cake and garnish with lemon wedges.

NOTE: Raw horseradish in the form of a root is sometimes available. Wash and peel the root and grate finely. Otherwise use bottled grated horseradish which should be rinsed, drained and squeezed dry.

MOSEL AUSLESE

Warm Seafood Salad with Green Chilli and Coriander

SERVES **6**

450g/1lb medium raw in-shell prawns, heads removed

1 × 170g/6oz tin of white crabmeat

1 tablespoon chopped coriander

110g/4oz unsalted roasted peanuts or cashew nuts, roughly chopped

salt and freshly ground black pepper

FOR THE MARINADE

2 tablespoons oil

finely grated zest of 1 lime

2 tablespoons lime juice

2 cloves of garlic, crushed

1 green chilli, finely chopped

½ teaspoon clear honey

2.5cm/1in piece of fresh ginger, peeled and grated

salt and freshly ground black pepper

TO SERVE

1 head of Chinese lettuce, finely shredded

4 tablespoons French dressing (see page 190)

1. Peel the prawns. Using a small sharp knife, slit along the back of each prawn and remove the black vein.

2. Mix together 1 tablespoon of the oil and all the remaining marinade ingredients. Add the prawns and leave to marinate for at least 30 minutes or overnight in the refrigerator.

3. Heat the remaining oil in a wok or heavy frying pan until smoking. Add the prawns and marinade and stir-fry for about 3 minutes or until the prawns have turned pink. Add the crabmeat, coriander and nuts and season to taste with salt and pepper. Toss the lettuce in the French dressing and serve immediately with the seafood on individual plates.

ALSACE GEWÜRZTRAMINER

WARM SEAFOOD SALAD WITH
GREEN CHILLI AND CORIANDER

LAMB CUTLETS WITH A
CORNMEAL CRUST AND
TOMATO AND MINT SALSA
(see page 94)

PEAR AND MASCARPONE PUFFS
(see page 152)

Grilled Tiger Prawns with Coriander Pesto

SERVES 6

24 large raw in-shell tiger prawns
1 tablespoon chilli oil
1 tablespoon lemon juice

FOR THE CORIANDER PESTO

1 large bunch of coriander
1 clove of garlic, peeled
30g/1oz blanched almonds
150ml/5fl oz olive oil
55g/2oz Parmesan cheese, freshly grated
salt and freshly ground black pepper

1. Using a small sharp knife, peel the tiger prawns, removing the heads but leaving the tails attached. Slit along the back of each prawn and remove the black vein. Put into a bowl and pour over the chilli oil and lemon juice. Leave to marinate for 1 hour.

2. Make the coriander pesto: chop the coriander roughly and put into a liquidizer with the garlic and almonds. Blend to a fine paste, then add the olive oil slowly, with the motor still running. Blend in the Parmesan cheese quickly and season to taste with salt and pepper.

3. Preheat a cast-iron grill pan or a heavy frying pan until smoking. Add the prawns and cook briefly on each side until pink.

4. To serve: put 4 prawns on to each of 6 individual plates with a heaped tablespoon of coriander pesto.

NOTE: If the pesto begins to look oily or grainy, add a tablespoon of cold water to prevent it from separating.

CHENIN BLANC

GRILLED TIGER PRAWNS
WITH CORIANDER PESTO

SMOKED CHICKEN AND
NOODLE SALAD
(see page 107)

FIGS WITH GOAT'S CHEESE AND
PECAN CARAMEL
(see page 162)

Scallops en Cocotte

SERVES 6

6 large fresh scallops

30g/1oz butter, melted

290ml/½ pint fish stock (see page 185) or court
*   bouillon (see page 186)*

3 eggs, separated

4 tablespoons double cream

a pinch of saffron strands

juice of ½ lemon

salt and freshly ground black pepper

1. Preheat the oven to 180°C/350°F/gas mark 4.

2. Prepare the scallops: remove the coral (roe) and muscle, reserving the coral.

3. Brush 6 ramekins with the butter.

4. Bring the stock or court bouillon to the boil in a saucepan, add the white scallop meat and immediately remove the pan from the heat. Cover and leave for about 3–5 minutes or until the scallops are just cooked.

5. Meanwhile, mix the egg yolks with the cream and saffron in a bowl. Push the scallop coral through a sieve into the mixture.

6. Remove the scallops from the stock and slice into quarters on the diagonal. Add to the bowl and season lightly with lemon juice, salt and pepper.

7. Whisk the egg whites to medium peaks and fold into the scallop mixture. Divide between the ramekins and cook in a bain-marie in the oven for 20 minutes or until just set. Serve immediately.

VERDICCHIO

↩

SCALLOPS EN COCOTTE

SPICED CHICKEN GOUJONS
WITH PINEAPPLE AND
CORIANDER SALSA
(see page 73)

CHOCOLATE BREAD AND
BUTTER PUDDING
(see page 153)

↩

Grilled Oysters

SERVES 6

36 oysters
290ml/½ pint single cream
Parmesan cheese
cayenne pepper
melted butter
dry breadcrumbs

1. Shuck the oysters: wrap a tea towel around your left hand. Place an oyster on your palm with the flat side upwards. Slip a short, wide-bladed kitchen or oyster shucking knife under the hinge and push it into the oyster. Press the middle fingers of your left hand on to the shell and with your right hand jerk up the knife and prise the two shells apart. Free the oyster from its base.

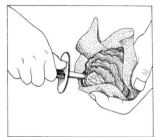

Slip a short kitchen or oyster knife under the hinge and push it into the oyster

2. Preheat the grill to its highest setting.

3. Rinse and dry the bottom shells, spoon a little cream into each and return the oysters. Sprinkle with Parmesan cheese, a very little cayenne, melted butter and dry breadcrumbs. Grill for 3–4 minutes or until hot and lightly browned. Serve immediately.

CHABLIS PREMIER CRU

GRILLED OYSTERS

BEEF STROGANOFF WITH GINGER
AND CHINESE FIVE-SPICE
(see page 89)

CITRUS FRUIT COMPOTE WITH
SPICED CARAMEL
(see page 163)

Ceviche

SERVES 6

675g/1½lb monkfish, halibut or salmon fillet,
  skinned and cut into thin slices or small strips
1 onion, thickly sliced
juice of 6 limes
2 tablespoons good-quality olive oil
a pinch of cayenne pepper
1 large green chilli, deseeded and cut into strips
  (optional)
2 tablespoons chopped dill
salt and freshly ground black pepper

1. Put the fish, onion, lime juice, oil, cayenne pepper, chilli and half the dill into a dish and leave to marinate in a cool place for 6 hours, giving an occasional stir. (If the fish is really thinly sliced, as little as 30 minutes will do; it is ready as soon as it looks 'cooked' – opaque rather than glassy.)

2. Remove the onion from the marinade. Season the fish with salt and pepper.

3. To serve: arrange the fish on a serving dish and sprinkle liberally with the remaining dill.

CHILEAN SAUVIGNON BLANC

CEVICHE

CALVES' LIVER WITH DRIED
CHERRY SAUCE
(see page 83)

PASSIONFRUIT AND MUSCAT
SYLLABUB
(see page 169)

Chilli Squid Salad

*Most fishmongers and supermarkets sell whole cleaned squid or
'tubes'. Try to buy the tentacles as well, as they add colour and
texture to the salad.*

SERVES 6

12 small squid, cleaned

3 green chillies, deseeded and finely chopped

1 tablespoon lemon juice

4 tablespoons olive oil

salt and freshly ground black pepper

FOR THE SALAD

18 cherry tomatoes, halved

½ cucumber, peeled, deseeded and cut into chunks

1 bunch of watercress

1 small bunch of rocket

salt and freshly ground black pepper

3 tablespoons French dressing (see page 190)

TO SERVE

1 × 70g/2½oz packet garlic croûtons

1. Using a sharp knife, score a diagonal pattern on the squid tubes. Keep the tentacles whole. Put into a bowl with the chillies, lemon juice and oil and leave to marinate for 30 minutes.

2. Heat a cast-iron grill pan until smoking and cook the squid briefly on both sides until golden-brown. Season lightly with salt and pepper.

3. Meanwhile, toss the salad ingredients together with the French dressing.

4. To serve: pile the salad on to 6 individual plates. Cut the squid into large rings and serve with the salad and croûtons.

AUSTRALIAN CHARDONNAY

CHILLI SQUID SALAD

GLAZED DUCK BREASTS WITH
APPLE AND SAGE CHUTNEY
(see page 80)

BAKED BANANAS IN
AMARETTI CRUMBLE
(see page 151)

Home-made Gravadlax with Pickled Cucumber

SERVES 6

675g/1½lb salmon fillet, skinned

85g/3oz caster sugar

85g/3oz coarse sea salt

finely grated zest of 1 lemon

1 large bunch of dill

FOR THE PICKLED CUCUMBER

1 large cucumber, peeled, deseeded and thinly sliced

2 tablespoons white wine vinegar

1 tablespoon caster sugar

1 tablespoon finely chopped dill

salt and freshly ground black pepper

1. Lay a large piece of clingfilm on a work surface and put the salmon fillet along one long side. Mix together the sugar, sea salt, lemon zest and dill and spread half the mixture on the surface of the fish, pressing down firmly. Flip the salmon over towards the centre of the clingfilm and press the remaining sugar/salt mixture on to the other side of the fish.

2. Wrap the salmon tightly in the clingfilm, place on a tray and refrigerate overnight.

3. The next day, wash the salmon fillet thoroughly and dry well. Using a sharp, thin-bladed knife, cut horizontal paper-thin slices from the salmon and arrange, overlapping, on 6 individual plates.

4. Make the pickled cucumber: mix all the ingredients together; season to taste with salt and pepper.

5. To serve: put a small mound of pickled cucumber beside each serving of gravadlax.

WHITE SANCERRE

HOME-MADE GRAVADLAX WITH
PICKLED CUCUMBER

STIR-FRIED BEEF WITH
SESAME PASTE

(see page 88)

GLAZED FRUITS AND CHESTNUTS
IN MADEIRA SYRUP

(see page 159)

Salmon Salad Tiède

SERVES 6

675g/1½lb salmon fillet, skinned

plain flour, seasoned with ground cumin

3 tablespoons olive oil

110g/4oz rindless streaky bacon, chopped

1 tablespoon sherry vinegar

salt and freshly ground black pepper

TO SERVE

mixed salad leaves

TO GARNISH

110g/4oz sun-dried tomatoes in oil, drained and
*   sliced*

85g/3oz Parmesan cheese, shaved with a vegetable
*   peeler*

sprigs of chervil

1. Cut the salmon fillet into strips the size of a little finger. Toss in the seasoned flour, pat off the excess and put on a plate in a single layer.

2. Heat the oil in a large frying pan, add the bacon and fry until crisp and brown. Remove from the pan with a slotted spoon and keep warm.

3. Cook the salmon strips, a few at a time, in the pan until lightly browned. Add the vinegar and shake the pan for a few seconds. Return the bacon to the pan, reheat, season to taste with salt and pepper and mix thoroughly.

4. To serve: put the salad leaves into a serving bowl, add the salmon mixture and toss lightly. Garnish with the sun-dried tomatoes, Parmesan cheese and chervil and serve immediately.

CALIFORNIAN ZINFANDEL ROSÉ

SALMON SALAD TIÈDE

CALVES' LIVER WITH
GINGER AND PECAN SAUCE
AND PARSNIP CRISPS
(see page 84)

HONEY AND FIG CUSTARDS
(see page 157)

Smoked Salmon on Potato and Buttermilk Pancakes

SERVES 6

340g/12oz smoked salmon

FOR THE PANCAKES

450g/1lb waxy potatoes, peeled and finely grated

225g/8oz plain flour

1 tablespoon caster sugar

½ teaspoon baking powder

½ teaspoon salt

290ml/½ pint buttermilk or milk soured with lemon juice

1 egg, beaten

2 tablespoons chopped dill

30g/1oz butter, melted

oil for frying

TO SERVE

150ml/5fl oz crème fraîche

TO GARNISH

sprigs of dill

1. Cut the smoked salmon into thin julienne strips and set aside.

2. Make the pancakes: pour boiling water over the grated potatoes in a bowl and leave to stand for 5 minutes. Sift together all the dry ingredients in a mixing bowl. Make a well in the centre, add the buttermilk or soured milk, egg, dill and butter and mix to a smooth batter. Drain the potatoes and stir into the batter.

3. Put enough oil into a large frying pan to just cover the base and heat until the oil is very hot. Drop tablespoonfuls of the potato mixture into the frying pan and turn the heat down to medium. Turn the pancakes when the tops are bubbling and the edges turning brown. Fry for 5 further minutes. Fry the remaining mixture in the same way.

4. To serve: reheat the pancakes if necessary and put 2 pancakes on to each of 6 individual plates. Pile on the smoked salmon strips and top with a heaped teaspoon of crème fraîche. Garnish with sprigs of dill and serve immediately.

CHAMPAGNE

SMOKED SALMON ON POTATO AND BUTTERMILK PANCAKES

STIR-FRIED CHICKEN WITH MANGO AND CORIANDER

(see page 77)

ROASTED COCONUT AND RUM CREAM

(see page 175)

Smoked Halibut with Japanese-style Cucumber Salad

SERVES 6

450g/1lb smoked halibut, thinly sliced

finely grated zest and juice of 2 limes

1 small cucumber

2 tablespoons white wine vinegar

2 teaspoons caster sugar

2 teaspoons light soy sauce

1 tablespoon chopped dill

3 tablespoons soured cream

salt and freshly ground white pepper

1. Put the smoked halibut into a shallow dish and add the lime zest and juice. Leave to marinate for 20–30 minutes.

2. Halve the cucumber lengthwise, scoop out the seeds with a teaspoon and cut into very thin strips 7.5cm/3in long. Combine the vinegar, sugar, soy sauce and dill and mix with the cucumber. Leave to stand for 5 minutes.

3. Stir the soured cream into the cucumber and season to taste with salt and pepper.

4. To serve: arrange the marinated smoked halibut on 6 individual plates and spoon a portion of cucumber salad beside each serving.

NEW ZEALAND CHARDONNAY

SMOKED HALIBUT WITH
JAPANESE-STYLE
CUCUMBER SALAD

HONEY-GLAZED ROAST
PARTRIDGES
(see page 81)

SUMMER RED FRUITS
MACERATED IN ELDERFLOWER
CORDIAL AND KIRSCH

(see page 164)

SOUFFLÉS

A perfectly risen soufflé is a brilliant way of getting a dinner party off to a really good start. Don't be daunted by the idea of making soufflés – they are much less temperamental than is often thought, especially individual ones. Soufflés can be made up well in advance and then frozen until needed. If you do this, add 5 minutes to the baking time. However, our shaded panels assume you are making the soufflés on the day of the dinner party.

Individual Red Onion and Rosemary Soufflés

SERVES 6

2 tablespoons oil
2 small red onions, finely chopped
1 tablespoon finely chopped rosemary
40g/1¼oz butter
dry white breadcrumbs
30g/1oz plain flour
¼ teaspoon dry English mustard
a pinch of cayenne pepper
220ml/7½fl oz milk
170g/6oz feta cheese, crumbled
3 eggs, separated
salt and freshly ground black pepper

INDIVIDUAL RED ONION AND ROSEMARY SOUFFLÉS

CHICKEN SAUTÉ WITH ARTICHOKES AND SUN-DRIED TOMATOES
(see page 75)

MARRON GLACÉ PUDDINGS
(see page 166)

---

1. Preheat the oven to 200°C/400°F/gas mark 6.

2. Heat the oil in a frying pan, add the onions and rosemary and sweat until the onions are soft but not coloured.

3. Melt the butter and use a little of it to brush 6 ramekins. Dust each ramekin with breadcrumbs, shaking out any excess.

4. Stir the flour, mustard and cayenne pepper into the remaining butter in a saucepan. Cook for 45 seconds. Blend in the milk and cook, stirring vigorously, for 2 minutes, until the mixture is very thick and leaves the sides of the pan. Remove from the heat.

5. Stir in the cheese, egg yolks and onion mixture. Season to taste: the mixture must be very well seasoned at this point.

6. Whisk the egg whites until stiff but not dry, and stir a spoonful into the cheese mixture, to loosen. Fold in the remainder and spoon into the ramekins until about two-thirds full. Run the tip of a knife around the top of the soufflé mixture. This will give a 'top-hat' appearance to the baked soufflé.

7. Put the ramekins on to a baking sheet and bake in the oven for 15 minutes until puffed up and golden. Give the soufflés a shake. If they wobble, bake for 5 further minutes.

AUSTRALIAN SHIRAZ

Twice-baked Individual Goat's Cheese Soufflés with Walnut and Parsley Sauce

SERVES 6

290ml/½ pint milk

1 slice of onion

45g/1½oz butter

45g/1½oz plain flour

110g/4oz soft goat's cheese, grated

a pinch of chopped thyme

3 eggs, separated

salt and freshly ground white pepper

TO SERVE

1 quantity walnut and parsley sauce (see page 194)

TWICE-BAKED INDIVIDUAL GOAT'S
CHEESE SOUFFLÉS WITH
WALNUT AND PARSLEY SAUCE

WARM PIGEON BREAST AND
CRACKED WHEAT SALAD
(see page 111)

CITRUS FRUIT COMPOTE WITH
SPICED CARAMEL
(see page 163)

---

1. Preheat the oven to 180°C/350°F/gas mark 4.

2. Heat the milk slowly with the onion in a saucepan. Remove from the heat and leave to infuse for 15 minutes, then strain.

3. Melt the butter and use a little of it to brush 6 ramekins or timbale moulds.

4. Stir the flour into the remaining butter in a saucepan. Cook, stirring, for 45 seconds. Gradually blend in the milk, off the heat, whisking until smooth.

5. Return to the heat and stir until the sauce boils and thickens. Remove from the heat, add the cheese, thyme, and egg yolks and season to taste with salt and pepper.

6. Whisk the egg whites until stiff but not dry and mix a spoonful into the mixture, to loosen. Fold in the remaining egg white. Spoon into the ramekins or timbales until two-thirds full.

7. Place in a roasting tin and pour in enough boiling water to come halfway up the sides. Bake in the oven for 15–20 minutes or until set. Remove and allow to sink and cool.

8. Turn the oven temperature up to 220°C/425°F/ gas mark 7.

9. Run a knife around the soufflés to loosen them. Turn them out into a shallow ovenproof dish. Warm the walnut and parsley sauce over a low heat and pour around the soufflés. Put into the oven for 10 minutes or until the tops are puffed up and golden. Give the soufflés a shake. If they wobble, bake for 5 further minutes. Serve immediately.

BROUILLY

Individual Cheese Soufflés

SERVES 6

40g/1¼oz butter

dry white breadcrumbs

30g/1oz plain flour

½ teaspoon made English mustard

a pinch of cayenne pepper

290ml/½ pint milk

85g/3oz strong Cheddar or Gruyère cheese, grated

4 eggs, separated

salt and freshly ground black pepper

1. Preheat the oven to 200°C/400°F/gas mark 6.

2. Melt the butter and use a little of it to brush 6 ramekins. Dust each ramekin with the breadcrumbs, shaking out any excess.

3. Stir the flour, mustard and cayenne pepper into the remaining butter in a saucepan. Cook for 45 seconds. Add the milk and cook, stirring vigorously, for 2 minutes until the mixture is very thick and leaves the sides of the pan. Remove from the heat.

4. Stir in the cheese, egg yolks, salt and pepper. Taste; the mixture should be very well seasoned.

5. Whisk the egg whites until stiff but not dry, and mix a spoonful into the mixture. Then fold in the rest and pour into the soufflé dish, which should be about two-thirds full. Run a knife-tip around the top of the soufflé mixture. This gives a 'top hat' appearance to the baked soufflé.

6. Place the ramekins on a baking sheet and bake in the oven for 15 minutes or until puffed up and golden. Give the soufflés a shake. If they wobble, bake for 5 further minutes.

CÔTES DU RHÔNE

❦

INDIVIDUAL CHEESE SOUFFLÉS

PUMPKIN AND PECAN PASTA
(see page 121)

WINTER FRUIT SALAD
(see page 174)

❦

MUSSEL AND SAFFRON BROTH

COUSCOUS SALAD WITH GRILLED AUBERGINES

SMOKED HALIBUT WITH JAPANESE-STYLE CUCUMBER SALAD

TWICE-BAKED INDIVIDUAL GOAT'S CHEESE SOUFFLÉS WITH WALNUT
AND PARSLEY SAUCE

MUSHROOM PARCELS

SALMON OLIVES WITH HERB SAUCE

GRILLED MACKEREL FILLETS WITH CUCUMBER AND FENNEL SALSA

SPICED CHICKEN GOUJONS WITH PINEAPPLE AND CORIANDER SALSA

Individual Arnold Bennett Soufflés

SERVES 6

1 slice of onion

1 bay leaf

4 black peppercorns

290ml/½ pint milk

225g/8oz smoked haddock

40g/1¼oz butter

dry white breadcrumbs

30g/1oz plain flour

½ teaspoon dry English mustard

1 tablespoon freshly grated Parmesan cheese

4 eggs, separated

freshly ground black pepper

1. Put the onion, bay leaf, peppercorns and milk into a large saucepan and heat slowly. When the milk is well flavoured, add the smoked haddock and poach gently for 10 minutes or until the fish is just cooked.

2. Drain the smoked haddock, reserving the milk. Skin, bone and flake the fish. Strain the milk and measure, making the quantity up to 290ml/½ pint with extra milk if necessary.

3. Preheat the oven to 200°C/400°F/gas mark 6.

4. Melt the butter and use a little of it to brush 6 ramekins. Dust each ramekin lightly with the breadcrumbs, shaking out any excess.

5. Stir the flour and mustard into the remaining butter in a saucepan and cook, stirring for 1 minute. Remove from the heat and gradually blend in the reserved milk. Return to the heat and bring slowly to the boil, stirring. Remove from the heat and stir in the flaked fish, cheese and egg yolks. Season to taste with pepper (the mixture will already be salty because of the smoked haddock).

6. Whisk the egg whites until stiff but not dry and mix a spoonful into the cheese mixture, to loosen. Carefully fold in the remaining egg white and spoon into the ramekins until about two-thirds full. Run the tip of a knife around the top of the soufflé mixture. This will give a 'top-hat' appearance to the baked soufflé.

7. Place the ramekins on a baking sheet and bake in the oven for 15–20 minutes. Check the soufflés after 15 minutes by giving them a slight shake. If they wobble, bake for a few more minutes. Serve immediately.

CALIFORNIAN SAUVIGNON BLANC

INDIVIDUAL ARNOLD BENNETT
SOUFFLÉS

FILLET OF LAMB WITH
SOY SAUCE, GINGER
AND GARLIC
(see page 95)

LEMON AND RASPBERRY CRÈMES
(see page 156)

MISCELLANEOUS FIRST COURSES

Sweet and Spicy Aubergine Kebabs

SERVES 6

3 small aubergines, cut into 1cm/½in cubes
salt
6 red onions, quartered
3 tablespoons medium sherry
1 tablespoon Dijon mustard
salt and freshly ground black pepper

FOR THE MARINADE

3 tablespoons clear honey
6 tablespoons balsamic vinegar
4 tablespoons sesame oil
juice of 1 lemon
a pinch of cayenne pepper
¼ teaspoon ground cumin
¼ teaspoon ground coriander

SWEET AND SPICY AUBERGINE

KEBABS

LEMON CHICKEN WITH

CREAM CHEESE AND HERBS

(see page 76)

CHESTNUT PUDDINGS

(see page 155)

TO SERVE

oakleaf lettuce or red chicory

6 tablespoons French dressing (see page 190)

1 large sprig of basil, chopped

1. Sprinkle the aubergine with salt and leave to drain in a colander for 30 minutes. Rinse thoroughly and dry on absorbent paper.

2. Mix together the marinade ingredients, pour over the aubergines and onions and stir carefully to coat the vegetables. Leave to marinate for at least 30 minutes or overnight.

3. Preheat the grill to its highest setting.
4. Thread the aubergine and onion alternately on to 12 kebab skewers, dividing each onion quarter in two. Grill for about 6 minutes on each side until thoroughly cooked and beginning to caramelize.
5. Meanwhile, put the marinade into a saucepan with the sherry and mustard and reduce, by boiling rapidly, until syrupy. Season to taste with salt and pepper.
6. To serve: toss the salad leaves in the French dressing and divide between 6 individual plates. Put 2 kebabs on to each plate. Pour over the sauce and sprinkle with the basil. Serve immediately.

BLANQUETTE DE LIMOUX

Spring Vegetables in Thai-style Dressing

SERVES 6

12 baby carrots, peeled and trimmed

8 baby corncobs

16 fine French beans, topped and tailed

4 baby courgettes

8 radishes, trimmed

12 sugar-snap peas, topped and tailed

85g/3oz broad beans, podded

12 spears of baby asparagus or sprue, cut into
  6cm/2½in pieces on the diagonal

FOR THE DRESSING

½ tablespoon Chinese five-spice powder

1 tablespoon lime juice

4 tablespoons grapeseed oil

½ small clove of garlic, crushed

1 tablespoon roughly chopped basil

1 tablespoon roughly chopped coriander

½ tablespoon sugar

salt and freshly ground black pepper

1. Cook the carrots in boiling salted water until just tender. Drain and refresh under running cold water.

2. Blanch each of the remaining vegetables separately in boiling salted water, and refresh them under running cold water. Remove the outer leathery skin from the broad beans.

3. Make the dressing: put the Chinese five-spice powder into a dry frying pan and cook over a high heat for a few minutes to bring out the flavour. Put into a liquidizer with the remaining dressing ingredients and blend until smooth.

4. Heat the dressing in a wok or a large frying pan, add all the vegetables and toss to coat with the dressing and heat through. Serve warm or cold.

ALSACE GEWÜRZTRAMINER

SPRING VEGETABLES IN
THAI-STYLE DRESSING

BAKED POUSSINS WITH
GARLIC AND LEMON
(see page 78)

CHOCOLATE RUM AND
RAISIN PUDDINGS
(see page 154)

Carrot Cakes with Spinach Sauce

SERVES 6

FOR THE SPINACH SAUCE

110g/4oz fresh spinach, cooked and chopped
150ml/5fl oz natural yoghurt
150g/5oz fromage frais
salt and freshly ground black pepper

FOR THE CARROT CAKES

30g/1oz butter
1 medium onion, finely chopped
2 teaspoons cumin seeds
2 tablespoons sesame seeds
340g/12oz carrots, peeled and coarsely grated
1 large parsnip, peeled and coarsely grated
30g/1oz fresh white breadcrumbs
1 tablespoon arrowroot or cornflour
salt and freshly ground black pepper
oil for frying

CARROT CAKES WITH

SPINACH SAUCE

SOLE FILLETS WITH FENNEL

AND CUMIN
(see page 69)

LEMON AND RASPBERRY

CRÈMES
(see page 156)

---

1. Make the spinach sauce: put the spinach, yoghurt and fromage frais into a food processor and blend to a smooth purée. Season to taste with salt and pepper, and set aside, covered, in the refrigerator.

2. Make the carrot cakes: melt the butter in a large frying pan over a low heat, add the onion and sweat until soft but not coloured. Toast the cumin and sesame seeds in a dry pan over a low heat until they start to pop.

3. Add the carrot and parsnip to the onion and cook over a low heat for a couple of minutes until slightly softened. Tip into a bowl and add the toasted seeds, breadcrumbs and arrowroot or cornflour. Season well with salt and pepper, divide into 6 equal portions and shape into flat cakes.

4. Heat enough oil to cover the bottom of the frying pan and fry the carrot cakes over a low heat, turning once, until a golden-brown crust has formed on both sides.

5. Serve very hot with the cold spinach sauce.

SOUTH AFRICAN CHENIN BLANC

Asparagus with Peanut Sauce

If you cannot find unsalted peanuts use cashew nuts and roast them lightly in the oven.

SERVES 6

1.1kg/2½lb young asparagus or sprue

FOR THE SAUCE

170g/6oz unsalted peanuts, roasted
4 tablespoons sunflower oil
1cm/½in piece of fresh ginger, peeled and grated
juice of 1 lemon
3 tablespoons light soy sauce
salt and freshly ground black pepper

1. Trim the asparagus of any woody parts.

2. Chop the peanuts roughly and mix with the remaining sauce ingredients. Season to taste with salt and pepper.

3. Meanwhile, cook the asparagus in a large saucepan of simmering salted water for about 4 minutes or until just tender. Drain thoroughly.

4. To serve: divide the asparagus between 6 individual plates, piling it up in the centre like a bonfire, and spoon over the peanut sauce.

SAUVIGNON DE TOURAINE

ASPARAGUS WITH PEANUT SAUCE

LOBSTER SALAD
(see page 103)

ALAIN SENDERENS' SOUPE AUX FRUITS EXOTIQUES
(see page 173)

Mushroom Parcels

Your guests open these aromatic parcels for themselves at the table.

SERVES 6

6 very large open-cap field mushrooms
1 small jar of artichoke paste, pesto or truffle paste
oil for brushing
2 cloves of garlic, crushed
3 tablespoons good-quality olive oil
3 tablespoons dry sherry
6 small sprigs of fresh thyme
salt and freshly ground black pepper

TO SERVE

110g/4oz Parmesan cheese, freshly grated
crusty French bread

1. Preheat the oven to 200°C/400°F/gas mark 6.

2. Trim the stalks from the mushrooms and spread the artichoke paste on the gills side of each. Cut 6 pieces of greaseproof paper, each large enough to wrap a mushroom, and brush the paper lightly with oil. Put a mushroom on each piece of paper, paste side up.

3. Divide the garlic between the mushrooms and sprinkle with the oil and sherry. Put a sprig of thyme on each mushroom, season with salt and pepper and fold up the paper to form a parcel.

4. Put the parcels on to a baking sheet and bake in the oven for 15–20 minutes. Serve immediately with the Parmesan cheese and bread handed separately.

RED CORBIÈRES

MUSHROOM PARCELS

DUCK BREASTS WITH ORIENTAL
PLUM SAUCE
(see page 79)

PASSIONFRUIT AND
MUSCAT SYLLABUB
(see page 169)

Spiced Mushroom Bruschetta

SERVES 6

100ml/3½fl oz good-quality olive oil

340g/12oz field mushrooms, thinly sliced

2 cloves of garlic, thinly sliced

½ teaspoon chilli powder

2 teaspoons dry English mustard

1 teaspoon garam masala

½ teaspoon salt

1 tablespoon chopped thyme

1 large ciabatta loaf, cut into 12 slices

TO GARNISH

150ml/5fl oz crème fraîche or soured cream

1 tablespoon snipped chives

1. Heat 2 tablespoons of the oil in a large frying pan, add the mushrooms and cook until soft, stirring frequently.

2. Heat the remaining oil slowly with the garlic in a small saucepan. Keep warm.

3. Preheat the grill to its highest setting.

4. Add the dry spices and thyme to the mushrooms and cook for 2–3 minutes.

5. Toast the ciabatta on both sides and brush one side liberally with the garlic-flavoured oil.

6. To serve: divide the mushroom mixture between the oiled side of the ciabatta slices and top with the crème fraîche and a sprinkling of chives. Serve immediately.

CHIANTI CLASSICO

**SPICED MUSHROOM
BRUSCHETTA**

**CHICKED SAUTÉ WITH
GREEN OLIVES**
(see page 74)

HONEY AND FIG CUSTARDS
(see page 157)

Mushrooms with Artichoke Hearts and Olives

SERVES 6

670g/1½lb button mushrooms, wiped and trimmed
110g/4oz green olives, pitted
1 × 400g/14oz tin of artichoke hearts, drained and
  quartered
290ml/½ pint water
4 tablespoons dry white vermouth
juice of ½ lemon
3 tablespoons extra virgin olive oil
1 sprig of sage
1 bay leaf
stick of celery, chopped
2 shallots, finely chopped
1 clove of garlic, crushed
a pinch of sugar
salt and freshly ground black pepper

TO GARNISH

30g/1oz Parmesan cheese, thinly shaved
1 tablespoon finely chopped coriander

1. Put all the ingredients except the mushrooms, olives, artichoke hearts, Parmesan and coriander into a large saucepan and bring to the boil. Reduce the heat, cover and simmer for 10 minutes. Remove and discard the sage and bay leaf.

2. Add the mushrooms to the pan and simmer for 10 minutes. Add the olives and artichoke hearts and simmer for 2 further minutes or until the sauce is syrupy. Season to taste with salt and pepper.

3. To serve: pile into a serving dish and sprinkle with Parmesan and coriander. Serve warm or cold.

WHITE VIN DE PAYS D'HÉRAULT

MUSHROOMS WITH ARTICHOKE
HEARTS AND OLIVES

COD STEAKS WITH A
SPICED CRUST
(see page 66)

CHOCOLATE BREAD AND
BUTTER PUDDING
(see page 153)

Goat's Cheese with Sesame Seeds and Thyme

SERVES 6

3 small goat's cheeses

2 eggs

110g/4oz dry white breadcrumbs

55g/2oz sesame seeds, toasted

2 tablespoons finely chopped thyme

salt and freshly ground black pepper

TO SERVE

1 head of frisée lettuce

1 bunch of watercress

3 tablespoons good-quality olive oil

1 tablespoon lemon juice

1. Cut the goat's cheeses in half horizontally. Beat the eggs lightly and put into a shallow dish. Mix the breadcrumbs with the sesame seeds and thyme and put into another dish. Season lightly with salt and pepper.

2. Dip the goat's cheese first into the egg and then into the breadcrumb mixture. Place on a baking sheet and refrigerate for 30 minutes.

3. Preheat the oven to 200°C/400°F/gas mark 6.

4. Bake the cheeses in the oven for 10–15 minutes or until soft.

5. Meanwhile, mix the lettuce and watercress in a large bowl. Whisk together the oil and lemon juice and season with salt and pepper. Add to the salad leaves and toss together thoroughly.

6. To serve: divide between 6 individual plates and put a half goat's cheese on each plate. Serve immediately.

SAINT-VÉRAN

GOAT'S CHEESE WITH SESAME
SEEDS AND THYME

LAMBS' KIDNEYS WITH
RED ONION AND SAGE
(see page 86)

WINTER FRUIT SALAD
(see page 174)

Parma Ham with Fig Chutney

SERVES 6

675g/1½lb Parma ham, thinly sliced

FOR THE CHUTNEY

1 tablespoon good-quality olive oil
6 shallots, peeled and quartered
a pinch of cayenne pepper
2 tablespoons port
1 tablespoon redcurrant jelly
6 ripe figs, quartered
salt and freshly ground black pepper

TO GARNISH

55g/2oz Parmesan cheese, thinly shaved

1. Make the chutney, heat the oil in a saucepan, add the shallots and sweat until soft but not coloured.

2. Add the cayenne, port and redcurrant jelly to the pan. Bring to the boil, then reduce the heat and simmer until syrupy.

3. Add the figs. Heat through and season to taste with salt and pepper.

4. To serve: arrange the Parma ham on 6 individual plates. Divide the fig chutney between the plates and garnish with shavings of Parmesan.

BANDOL ROSÉ

↪

PARMA HAM WITH FIG CHUTNEY

CHICKEN BREASTS STUFFED WITH OLIVE AND CAPER TAPENADE

(see page 71)

BAKED BANANAS IN AMARETTI CRUMBLE

(see page 151)

↪

Individual Smoked Chicken Rösti

SERVES 6

1 smoked chicken

55g/2oz butter

1 onion, finely chopped

4 rashers of rindless streaky bacon, chopped

2 parsnips, peeled and grated

1 clove of garlic, crushed

salt and freshly ground black pepper

TO GARNISH

radicchio leaves

French dressing (see page 190)

1. Skin and bone the chicken and pull the breast meat into short strips. Put the remaining dark meat, all bones and sinews removed, into a food processor and chop finely.

2. Preheat the oven to 200°C/400°F/gas mark 6.

3. Heat the butter in a large ovenproof frying pan, add the onion and sweat until soft but not coloured. Add the bacon and continue to cook until beginning to brown. Add the parsnips and garlic and cook over a low heat until the parsnip is soft. Remove from the heat. Add all the chicken, season to taste with salt and pepper and mix thoroughly, divide the mixture into 6 equal portions and form into flat cakes.

4. Put on to a greased baking sheet and bake in the oven for 15 minutes or until golden-brown.

5. To serve: toss the radicchio in the French dressing and divide between 6 individual plates. Add the rösti and serve immediately.

ALSACE RIESLING

INDIVIDUAL SMOKED CHICKEN RÖSTI

MONKFISH SALAD WITH GREEN SAUCE

(see page 105)

APPLES WITH CARAMELIZED CRESCENTS

(see page 160)

MAIN COURSES

FISH

Stir-fried Prawns with Coriander

This is a favourite stir-fried recipe at Leith's School. It was originally demonstrated to us by Yan-Kit So.

SERVES 6

1.35kg/3lb medium raw in-shell prawns, heads removed
2 tablespoons sunflower oil
2 cloves of garlic, crushed
5cm/2in piece of fresh root ginger, peeled and grated
3 tablespoons dry sherry
1 bunch spring onions, chopped
4 tablespoons chopped coriander

FOR THE MARINADE

1½ teaspoons salt
3 teaspoons sugar
3 tablespoons light soy sauce
6 teaspoons Worcestershire sauce
3 teaspoons sunflower oil
freshly ground black pepper

1. Peel the prawns. Using a small sharp knife, slit along the back of each prawn and remove the black vein. Cut off the legs. Wash and pat dry.

2. Mix together all the marinade ingredients and add the prawns. Leave to marinate for at least 30 minutes or overnight in the refrigerator.

3. Heat a wok, add the oil, and when fairly hot add the garlic and ginger.
4. Add the prawns to the wok. Spread them out in a single layer and fry for about 1 minute. Reduce the heat if they begin to burn. Turn over and fry on the other side for about 1 minute. Turn up the heat if necessary. Splash in the sherry. The prawns are cooked when they have turned red and curled up. Sprinkle with the spring onion and coriander. Stir once or twice and serve immediately.

NEW ZEALAND RIESLING

࿚

WARM PUY LENTIL SALAD

(see page 15)

STIR-FRIED PRAWNS WITH CORIANDER

CHESTNUT PUDDINGS

(see page 155)

࿚

Salmon Olives with Herb Sauce

SERVES 6

3 × 270g/10oz salmon tail fillets, skinned
oil for brushing
juice of 1 lemon
3 tablespoons dry white wine
salt and freshly ground black pepper
1 bay leaf
3 cloves of garlic, unpeeled
oil
55g/2oz dry white breadcrumbs
finely grated zest of 3 limes
3 tablespoons finely chopped dill
salt and freshly ground black pepper

FOR THE HERB SAUCE

6 tablespoons good-quality olive oil
2 tablespoons white wine vinegar
2 tablespoons finely chopped dill
2 tablespoons finely chopped parsley
1 teaspoon Dijon mustard

FOR THE GARNISH

sprigs of dill
lime wedges

CUCUMBER AND MELON
GAZPACHO

(see page 7)

SALMON OLIVES WITH
HERB SAUCE

MACERATED STRAWBERRIES

(see page 165)

1. Preheat the oven to 200°C/400°F/gas mark 6.

2. Trim the salmon fillets and remove any bones. Slice each salmon fillet in half horizontally. Put each slice between 2 pieces of clingfilm and bat them out carefully with a rolling pin or heavy saucepan to increase the size by about a quarter.

3. Place the cloves of garlic on a baking sheet, brush with a little oil and bake in the oven for about 10 minutes until soft. Peel and crush the garlic and mix with the breadcrumbs, lime zest and dill. Season to taste with salt and pepper.

4. Divide the mixture between the 6 slices of salmon and roll them up towards the narrow end. Secure the salmon olives with a cocktail stick.

5. Put the salmon olives on to a large sheet of lightly oiled kitchen foil and brush with oil. Sprinkle with the lemon juice and white wine and season lightly. Add the bay leaf and fold up the edges of the foil to form a loosely wrapped but securely sealed parcel. Put on to a baking sheet and bake in the oven for 10 minutes.

6. Meanwhile, make the herb sauce: combine all the ingredients in a liquidizer or food processor and process until smooth.

7. When the salmon olives are cooked, add 2 tablespoons of the hot cooking liquid from the parcel to the sauce and process again briefly. Season to taste with salt and pepper.
8. Lift the salmon olives from the foil, drain and cut each olive in half on the diagonal.
9. To serve: flood 6 plates with the herb sauce and put 2 pieces of salmon on each plate. Garnish each with a sprig of dill and a lime wedge.

NEW ZEALAND SAUVIGNON BLANC

Salmon Fillet with Vodka and Lime

SERVES 6

1.1kg/2½lb salmon, skinned and filleted
oil for brushing
2 bay leaves
5 tablespoons vodka
finely grated zest and juice of 1 lime
salt and freshly ground black pepper

FOR THE SAUCE

2 bunches of watercress, roughly chopped
255g/9oz fromage frais
2 tablespoons double cream
salt and freshly ground black pepper

1. Put a baking sheet into the oven and preheat the oven to 200°C/400°F/gas mark 6.

2. Trim the salmon fillet and remove any bones.

3. Lightly oil a large sheet of kitchen foil and put the salmon fillet, skinned side down, in the centre of the sheet. Add the bay leaves, vodka, lime zest and juice and season lightly with salt and pepper. Wrap the salmon loosely in the foil, sealing the edges tightly. Refrigerate for 30 minutes.

4. Place the salmon parcel on the hot baking sheet and bake in the centre of the oven for 25 minutes.

5. Meanwhile, make the sauce: put the watercress, fromage frais and cream into a liquidizer or food processor and process until smooth. Season to taste with salt and pepper.

6. Remove the salmon from the foil and serve with the sauce handed separately in a sauce-boat.

POUILLY-FUISSÉ

〜

ASPARAGUS WITH PEANUT SAUCE

(see page 47)

SALMON FILLET WITH VODKA AND LIME

ALAIN SENDERENS' SOUPE AUX FRUITS EXOTIQUES

(see page 173)

〜

Salmon Baked with a Sweet and Hot Crust

SERVES 6

1.1kg/2½lb salmon fillet, skinned
oil for brushing

FOR THE CRUST

1 tablespoon demerara sugar
½ teaspoon dry English mustard
finely grated zest of 3 limes or 2 lemons
2 tablespoons grainy mustard
6 tablespoons dried breadcrumbs
a pinch of cayenne pepper

TO GARNISH

watercress

1. Preheat the oven to 190°C/375°F/gas mark 5.

2. Trim the salmon fillet and remove any bones.

3. Mix together the crust ingredients.

4. Press over the salmon. Cut into 6 even pieces, place on a lightly oiled baking sheet and bake in the oven for 15 minutes.

5. Garnish the salmon with bouquets of watercress and serve immediately.

CHABLIS

INDIVIDUAL RED ONION AND
ROSEMARY SOUFFLÉS
(see page 40)

SALMON BAKED WITH A
SWEET AND HOT CRUST

HONEY AND FIG CUSTARDS
(see page 157)

Salmon Steaks with Oyster Mushroom and Whisky Sauce

SERVES 6

6 × 170g/6oz salmon steaks

1 tablespoon oil

salt and freshly ground black pepper

FOR THE SAUCE

55g/2oz butter

450g/1lb oyster mushrooms, roughly torn

5 tablespoons whisky

1 rounded tablespoon grainy mustard

290ml/½ pint double cream

salt and freshly ground black pepper

1. Preheat the grill to its highest setting.

2. Trim the salmon steaks and remove any small bones.

3. Brush with oil and season lightly with salt and pepper. Grill for 7–10 minutes, turning once.

4. Meanwhile make the sauce: heat the butter in a large frying pan, add the mushrooms and cook for 2–3 minutes or until soft. Add the whisky and boil until reduced by half. Add the mustard and cream and boil again until thickened. Season to taste with salt and pepper.

5. Serve the salmon immediately with the mushroom and whisky sauce handed separately in a sauce-boat.

AUSTRALIAN SEMILLON

COUSCOUS SALAD WITH
GRILLED AUBERGINES

(see page 14)

SALMON STEAKS WITH OYSTER
MUSHROOM AND WHISKY SAUCE

PASSIONFRUIT AND MUSCAT
SYLLABUB

(see page 169)

Grilled Mackerel Fillets with Cucumber and Fennel Salsa

SERVES 6

6 × 225g/8oz mackerel fillets

finely grated zest and juice of 2 limes

2 tablespoons balsamic vinegar

FOR THE CUCUMBER AND FENNEL SALSA

2 bulbs of fennel

1 cucumber, peeled, deseeded and diced

juice of 1 lime

4 tablespoons extra virgin olive oil

2 tablespoons chopped chervil

salt and freshly ground black pepper

1. Remove as many bones as possible from the mackerel fillets and make diagonal slashes in the skin. Put into a shallow dish in one layer, skin side up, and pour over the lime juice and zest and the vinegar. Cover and marinate overnight in the refrigerator.

2. Make the salsa: remove any tough outer leaves from the fennel and cut into fine dice. Blanch in a saucepan of boiling salted water and refresh under running cold water. Mix with the remaining salsa ingredients. Season to taste with salt and pepper.

3. Preheat the grill to its highest setting. Remove the mackerel from the marinade and put the fillets on the grill pan, skin side up. Grill for 2 minutes, then turn down the heat and continue grilling for about 5–6 minutes until the mackerel is cooked.

4. To serve: put a mackerel fillet on to each of 6 individual plates. Spoon a portion of the fennel and cucumber salsa beside each fillet.

WHITE RIOJA

༞

ROASTED SWEET PEPPER SOUP

(see page 8)

GRILLED MACKEREL FILLETS
WITH CUCUMBER AND FENNEL
SALSA

LEMON CURD ICE CREAM

(see page 172)

༞

Red Snapper with Tomato and Olive Concasse

SERVES 6

6 × 225g/8oz red snapper fillets

3 tablespoons finely chopped thyme

150ml/5fl oz balsamic vinegar

150ml/¼ pint olive oil

6 large ripe tomatoes, peeled and deseeded

170g/6oz pitted black olives

salt and freshly ground black pepper

1. Trim the red snapper fillets and remove any bones. Put the fillets into a shallow ovenproof dish.

2. Mix together 1 tablespoon of the thyme, the vinegar and oil and pour over the fish. Leave to marinate for 1 hour or overnight.

3. Meanwhile, dice the tomatoes and black olives and mix together with the remaining thyme.

4. Preheat the oven to 200°C/400°F/gas mark 6.

5. Season the snapper fillets with salt and pepper and bake in the oven for 5–10 minutes or until cooked.

6. To serve: lift the snapper fillets from the cooking liquid and put on to a serving plate. Mix the tomatoes and black olives with the cooking liquid, season to taste with salt and pepper and pour over the snapper.

ROSÉ DE PROVENCE

THREE-CHEESE PÂTÉ
WITH PECANS

(see page 26)

RED SNAPPER WITH TOMATO
AND OLIVE CONCASSE

NECTARINE, STRAWBERRY
AND ALMOND SPONGE

(see page 150)

Crusted Cod Steaks with Rocket Paste

SERVES 6

6 × 170g/6oz cod steaks
4 tablespoons olive oil
2 lemons, quartered

FOR THE ROCKET PASTE

55g/2oz rocket
55g/2oz blanched almonds
70ml/3fl oz olive oil
55g/2oz Parmesan cheese, freshly grated
salt and freshly ground black pepper

FOR THE CRUST

55g/2oz Parmesan cheese, grated
55g/2oz dry white breadcrumbs
salt and freshly ground black pepper

TO GARNISH

lemon wedges

1. Trim the cod steaks and remove any small bones. Put the steaks into a large shallow ovenproof dish in a single layer. Pour over the oil and squeeze over some of the juice from the lemon quarters. Tuck the lemon quarters around the fish, cover and marinate overnight in the refrigerator.

2. Make the rocket paste: put all the ingredients into a liquidizer and process until smooth. Season to taste with salt and pepper. If the paste begins to look oily and too thick, add 1 tablespoon water to the mixture.

3. Preheat the oven to 200°C/400°F/gas mark 6.

4. Mix together the Parmesan cheese and breadcrumbs, season to taste with salt and pepper and sprinkle over the cod steaks. Bake in the oven for 12–15 minutes or until the crust is golden-brown and the fish cooked.

5. To serve: place a cod steak on each of 6 individual plates. Drizzle over a little of the cooking liquid and spoon a portion of rocket paste beside each steak. Garnish with a lemon wedge.

ENTRE-DEUX-MERS

ROAST AUBERGINE DIP
(see page 23)

ROAST GARLIC DIP
(see page 24)

OLIVE AND CHILLI DIP
(see page 25)

CRUSTED COD STEAKS WITH
ROCKET PASTE

BAKED BANANAS IN
AMARETTI CRUMBLE
(see page 151)

Individual Cod Gratins

SERVES 6

900g/2lb cod fillet, skinned

30g/1oz butter

6 small leeks, white part only, thickly sliced

salt and freshly ground black pepper

290ml/½ pint dry white wine

425ml/¾ pint fish stock (see page 185)

150ml/5fl oz double cream

2 tablespoons grainy mustard

3 tablespoons chopped parsley

170g/6oz Gruyère cheese, grated

2 tablespoons dry white breadcrumbs

1. Preheat the oven to 200°C/400°F/gas mark 6.

2. Trim the cod fillet, remove any bones and cut into 2.5cm/1in cubes and divide between 6 individual gratin dishes.

3. Melt the butter in a large saucepan, add the leeks and sweat until soft but not coloured. Season to taste with salt and pepper and divide between the gratin dishes.

4. Put the wine into the saucepan and reduce by boiling rapidly to a quarter of its original quantity. Add the stock and reduce again by half. Finally, add the double cream and reduce by half. Stir the sauce every so often to prevent the cream from catching on the bottom of the pan.

5. Add the mustard and parsley and season to taste with salt and pepper. Divide the sauce between the gratin dishes and sprinkle over the cheese and breadcrumbs.

6. Bake in the oven for 15 minutes or until the top is golden-brown and bubbling.

WHITE SAUMUR

⌐⌐

**SPINACH AND BACON SALAD
WITH RED CHILLI AND MANGO**
(see page 20)

INDIVIDUAL COD GRATINS

**CHOCOLATE BREAD AND
BUTTER PUDDING**
(see page 153)

⌐⌐

Cod Steaks with a Spiced Crust

SERVES 6

6 × 170g/6oz cod steaks

FOR THE CRUST

½ teaspoon chilli powder

1 teaspoon caster sugar

2 teaspoons dry English mustard

1½ teaspoons garam masala

½ teaspoon salt

55g/2oz butter, melted

55g/2oz dry white breadcrumbs

55g/2oz unsalted peanuts, finely chopped

55g/2oz cashew nuts, finely chopped

TO SERVE

lemon wedges

1. Preheat the oven to 190°C/375°F/gas mark 5.

2. Trim the cod steaks and remove any small bones.

3. Put the steaks into an ovenproof serving dish.

4. Mix together all the crust ingredients and divide between the steaks, pressing down firmly.

5. Bake the cod steaks in the oven for 12–15 minutes or until the fish is cooked and the crust golden-brown. Serve immediately with the lemon wedges.

POUILLY FUMÉ

PARMA HAM WITH FIG CHUTNEY

(see page 52)

COD STEAKS WITH
A SPICED CRUST

ROASTED COCONUT AND
RUM CREAM
(see page 175)

Halibut Steaks with Cashew Nuts and Cheese

SERVES 6

6 × 170g/6oz halibut steaks
100ml/3½fl oz sunflower oil
juice of 2 lemons
1 large sprig of thyme
15g/½oz butter, melted

FOR THE CRUST

110g/4oz cashew nuts, chopped
55g/2oz Cheddar cheese, grated
1 tablespoon chopped thyme
55g/2oz dry white breadcrumbs
2 tablespoons Dijon mustard
salt and freshly ground black pepper

TO SERVE

lemon wedges

1. Trim the halibut steaks and remove any small bones. Put the steaks into a shallow dish in a single layer. Pour over the oil and lemon juice and break the thyme over the fish. Cover and marinate overnight in the refrigerator.

2. Make the crust: mix together the nuts, cheese, thyme, breadcrumbs and mustard. Season to taste with salt and pepper.

3. Preheat the grill to its medium setting. Brush a baking sheet with the melted butter, lift the halibut from the marinade and place on the baking sheet. Sprinkle the crust mixture over the fish, pressing down firmly. Grill for about 5–10 minutes or until the fish is cooked and the crust golden-brown. Serve with the lemon wedges.

WHITE RULLY

SPICED OLIVE AND CHERRY
TOMATO SALAD

(see page 16)

HALIBUT STEAKS WITH CASHEW
NUTS AND CHEESE

GLAZED FRUITS AND CHESTNUTS
IN MADEIRA SYRUP

(see page 159)

Halibut with Caramelized Chicory

SERVES 6

6 × 170g/6oz halibut steaks

1 tablespoon olive oil

110g/4oz shallots, thinly sliced

3 large heads of chicory

1 tablespoon clear honey

2 tablespoons capers, rinsed and drained

salt and freshly ground black pepper

FOR THE MARINADE

2 tablespoons dry white wine

2 tablespoons white wine vinegar

3 tablespoons hazelnut oil

freshly ground black pepper

CUCUMBER AND MELON

GAZPACHO

(see page 7)

HALIBUT WITH CARAMELIZED

CHICORY

MANGO, RASPBERRY AND

BLUEBERRY CLAFOUTIS

(see page 149)

---

1. Trim the halibut steaks and remove any bones. Put the steaks into a shallow dish.

2. Whisk together all the marinade ingredients and pour over the halibut steaks. Cover and leave to marinate overnight in the refrigerator.

3. Heat the oil in a large frying pan, add the shallots and cook until soft but not coloured. Cut the chicory in half lengthwise and remove part of the hard core in the centre, taking care to keep the leaves attached. Add the chicory to the pan, cut side down, and fry gently until beginning to soften.

4. Preheat the grill to medium.

5. Lift the halibut steaks from the marinade and place in a single layer on a large baking sheet. Grill for about 6–8 minutes, depending on their thickness, until cooked, turning once.

6. Meanwhile, pour the marinade on to the chicory, add the honey and capers and bring to the boil. Simmer gently until the chicory are soft and the marinade is a syrupy consistency. Season to taste with salt and pepper.

7. Remove the halibut from the cooking juices and keep warm. Strain the cooking juices into the sauce and continue to simmer until slightly thickened.

8. To serve: place a halibut steak on each of 6 individual plates and spoon over the chicory and sauce.

AUSTRALIAN CHARDONNAY

Sole Fillets with Fennel and Cumin

SERVES 6

6 small lemon sole, filleted and skinned

2 bulbs of fennel

plain flour seasoned with salt, freshly ground black
*   pepper and ground cumin*

110g/4oz unsalted butter

1 teaspoon ground cumin

4 tablespoons dry white wine

2 tablespoons capers, rinsed and drained

55g/2oz pinenuts, toasted

lemon juice

salt and freshly ground black pepper

1. Trim the lemon sole fillets, remove any bones and set aside.

2. Remove any tough outer leaves from the fennel. Cut each bulb into 8, trimming away most of the core, leaving just enough to hold the wedges together.

3. Blanch the fennel in a saucepan of boiling salted water for 2 minutes. Drain, refresh under running cold water and dry well. Set aside.

4. Coat the sole fillets with the seasoned flour, patting off any excess.

5. Heat 55g/2oz of the butter in a large frying pan until foaming. Add as many sole fillets as will fit comfortably in the pan and fry for about 30 seconds on each side. Remove from the pan and keep warm while frying the remaining fillets in the same way. Keep all the sole fillets warm.

6. Wipe any burnt sediment from the pan and melt the remaining butter. Add the fennel and cumin and fry until golden-brown. Add the wine, capers and pinenuts and cook until bubbling. Season to taste with lemon juice, salt and pepper.

7. To serve: arrange the sole fillets on 6 individual plates. Spoon over the vegetables and pour over the sauce. Serve immediately.

MUSCADET DE SÈVRE-ET-MAINE SUR LIE

PROSCIUTTO AND CANNELLINI
BEAN SOUP
(see page 12)

SOLE FILLETS WITH FENNEL
AND CUMIN

RUBY RED FRUIT PARCELS
(see page 158)

Monkfish on Rosemary Skewers

SERVES 6

1.35kg/3lb monkfish, filleted and skinned
6 small courgettes
6 baby aubergines
12 × 15cm/6in branches of rosemary

FOR THE MARINADE

6 tablespoons olive oil
1 tablespoon chilli sauce
1 tablespoon grainy mustard

1. Cut the monkfish into 36 even pieces. Cut each courgette into 6 × 2cm/1in lengths and halve each aubergine horizontally.

2. Prepare the skewers: remove the leaves from the rosemary, leaving 2cm/1in of leaves at the top. Chop the leaves roughly and add to the marinade ingredients. Mix thoroughly.

3. Put the monkfish, courgettes and aubergines into the marinade and leave for at least 30 minutes or overnight.

4. Preheat the grill to its highest setting.
5. Thread each rosemary skewer alternately with the monkfish, courgette and aubergine.
6. Lay the skewers on a large grill pan in a single layer. Grill for 7–10 minutes, turning frequently, until the fish and vegetables are cooked.

NOTE: These are delicious cooked on a barbecue.

To achieve the full aroma, strip the monkfish off the rosemary skewers at the table. Metal or wooden skewers (soaked to prevent burning) may also be used, in which case try to use rosemary in the marinade.

CHILLED BEAUJOLAIS

ROAST SWEET PEPPER SOUP
(see page 8)

MONKFISH ON ROSEMARY SKEWERS

PEAR AND MASCARPONE PUFFS
(see page 152)

POULTRY, GAME AND OFFAL

Chicken Breasts Stuffed with Olive and Caper Tapenade

SERVES 6

6 chicken breasts, skinned and boned

FOR THE TAPENADE

85g/3oz green olives, pitted
30g/1oz capers, rinsed and drained
1 bunch of parsley
30g/1oz blanched almonds
4 anchovy fillets, drained
150ml/5fl oz olive oil
salt and freshly ground black pepper

SPICED MUSHROOM BRUSCHETTA

(see page 49)

CHICKEN BREASTS STUFFED
WITH OLIVE AND CAPER
TAPENADE

PASSIONFRUIT AND MUSCAT
SYLLABUB

(see page 169)

---

1. Preheat the oven to 200°C/400°F/gas mark 6.

2. Trim the chicken of any fat. Make a pocket in each chicken breast by cutting horizontally through the meat, almost to the other side.

3. Make the tapenade: put the olives, capers and parsley into a liquidizer or food processor and process to a paste. Add the almonds and anchovy fillets and process again briefly. Add the oil slowly, with the motor still running, and season to taste with salt and pepper.

4. Divide the tapenade into 6 even portions, stuff each chicken breast and secure the edges with cocktail sticks.

5. Season the chicken with salt and pepper and put into an ovenproof serving dish. Cook on the top shelf of the oven for 20–30 minutes until cooked through. Remove the cocktail sticks and serve straight from the dish.

WHITE RIOJA

Grilled Chicken with Mustard and Cranberries

SERVES 6

6 chicken breasts, skinned and boned

55g/2oz butter, softened

2 tablespoons grainy mustard

finely grated zest and juice of 2 oranges

salt and freshly ground black pepper

340g/1lb cranberries, fresh or frozen

1 tablespoon finely chopped thyme

8 spring onions, sliced

150ml/5fl oz chicken stock (see page 185) or water

85g/3oz plus 1 tablespoon demerara sugar

55g/2oz dried breadcrumbs

¼ teaspoon chilli flakes

1. Preheat the oven to 200°C/400°F/gas mark 6.

2. Trim the chicken of any fat.

3. Mix together half the butter, the mustard and the zest of 1 orange. Spread the underside of the chicken breasts with half the mixture and put into a roasting tin, plain side down.

4. Season with salt and pepper and sprinkle with a little of the orange juice. Cook in the oven for 5 minutes.

5. Turn the chicken over and spread with the remaining butter mixture. Season with salt and pepper and sprinkle with a little more of the orange juice. Cook for 10 further minutes.

6. Meanwhile, put the cranberries, thyme, spring onions, stock or water and 85g/3oz of the sugar and the remaining orange juice into a saucepan. Bring to the boil and reduce by boiling rapidly until syrupy.

7. Season to taste with salt and pepper and keep warm.

8. Preheat the grill to its medium setting.

9. Melt the remaining butter and mix with the breadcrumbs, chilli flakes and the remaining orange zest and sugar. Sprinkle over the cooked chicken breasts and grill until golden-brown. Serve immediately with the cranberry sauce handed separately in a sauce-boat.

CHIROUBLES

↩

SMOKED HALIBUT PÂTÉ

(see page 27)

GRILLED CHICKEN WITH
MUSTARD AND CRANBERRIES

LEMON AND RASPBERRY
CRÈMES

(see page 156)

↩

Spiced Chicken Goujons with Pineapple and Coriander Salsa

Make the salsa while the chicken strips are chilling.

SERVES 6

6 large chicken breasts, skinned and boned

2 cloves of garlic, crushed

150ml/5fl oz natural yoghurt

110g/4oz dry white breadcrumbs

finely grated zest of 1 lemon

½ green chilli, deseeded and finely chopped

8 tablespoons sesame seeds

salt and freshly ground black pepper

150ml/5fl oz sunflower oil

1 quantity pineapple and coriander salsa (see page 195)

SALMON RILLETTES

(see page 28)

SPICED CHICKEN GOUJONS WITH PINEAPPLE AND CORIANDER SALSA

A SELECTION OF CHEESES

(see page 176)

1. Cut the chicken into strips and mix with the garlic and yoghurt.

2. Mix together the breadcrumbs, lemon zest, chilli and sesame seeds and spread out on a large plate. Season lightly with salt and pepper. Coat the chicken strips with the breadcrumb mixture and pat off any excess. Put the chicken strips on a plate in a single layer without touching each other and refrigerate for 15 minutes to firm the chicken up.

3. Heat the oil in a large frying pan until a cube of bread sizzles and rises to the top. Fry the chicken pieces in batches, taking care not to overcrowd the pan. Drain well on absorbent paper. Sprinkle with salt.

4. Serve hot on individual plates, with a portion of pineapple and coriander salsa beside each serving.

ALSACE GEWÜRZTRAMINER

Chicken Sauté with Green Olives

SERVES 6

6 chicken breasts, skinned and boned

4 tablespoons sultanas

4 tablespoons dry white wine

2 tablespoons olive oil

1 Spanish onion, finely chopped

6 cloves of garlic, crushed

1 teaspoon ground cinnamon

6 tablespoons balsamic vinegar

55g/2oz green olives, pitted

salt and freshly ground black pepper

2 tablespoons sunflower seeds, toasted (optional)

1. Preheat the oven to 190°C/375°F/gas mark 5.

2. Slice the chicken into bite-sized pieces.

3. Soak the sultanas in the wine.

4. Heat half the oil in a large, heavy-bottomed frying pan. Add the chicken pieces and fry, turning, until golden-brown. Remove from pan, add the onion and garlic and fry until lightly browned. Add the cinnamon and cook briefly. Return the chicken to the pan, cover and cook over a gentle heat for about 15 minutes or until cooked.

5. Remove the chicken and vegetables from the pan and keep warm. Tip off any fat and add the vinegar, scraping any sediment from the bottom of the pan. Add the sultanas, wine and olives. Reduce by boiling rapidly until syrupy. Add any juices from the chicken. Season to taste.

6. To serve: put the chicken pieces on to a serving dish and surround with the vegetables. Sprinkle over the sunflower seeds, if used. Hand the sauce separately in a sauce-boat.

PENEDÈS ESMERELDA

SMOKED SALMON ON POTATO
AND BUTTERMILK PANCAKES

(see page 38)

CHICKEN SAUTÉ WITH
GREEN OLIVES

A SELECTION OF CHEESES

(see page 176)

Chicken Sauté with Artichokes and Sun-dried Tomatoes

SERVES 6

6 large chicken breasts, skinned and boned

plain flour seasoned with salt and cayenne pepper

½ tablespoon oil

110g/4oz pancetta or rindless streaky bacon,
  chopped

5 tablespoons dry white vermouth

1 × 400g/14oz tin of artichoke hearts, drained and
  halved

55g/2oz sun-dried tomatoes in oil, drained and
  sliced

1 tablespoon finely chopped sage

salt and freshly ground black pepper

TO GARNISH

30g/1oz pinenuts, toasted

1. Trim the chicken breasts of any fat and cut into bite-sized pieces. Toss in the seasoned flour and shake off any excess. Put the chicken pieces on to a plate in a single layer, without touching each other.

2. Heat the oil in a large frying pan, add the pancetta or bacon and fry until brown. Remove from the pan with a slotted spoon and keep warm.

3. Add the chicken pieces, a few at a time, to the hot pan and fry, turning, until golden-brown and cooked through. Keep warm with the pancetta or bacon.

4. Add 2 tablespoons water to the pan and bring to the boil, then add the vermouth. Reduce by boiling rapidly until syrupy. Return the pancetta or bacon and the chicken to the pan together with the artichoke hearts, sun-dried tomatoes and sage. Reheat and season to taste with salt and pepper.

CALIFORNIAN CHARDONNAY

TWICE-BAKED INDIVIDUAL GOAT'S
CHEESE SOUFFLÉS WITH
WALNUT AND PARSLEY SAUCE

(see page 41)

CHICKEN SAUTÉ
WITH ARTICHOKES AND
SUN-DRIED TOMATOES

MARRON GLACÉ PUDDINGS

(see page 166)

Lemon Chicken with Cream Cheese and Herbs

SERVES 6

6 large chicken breasts, skinned and boned

4 tablespoons good-quality olive oil

finely grated zest of 2 lemons

3 sprigs of rosemary, chopped

140g/5oz packet of cream cheese with herbs

salt and freshly ground black pepper

2 tablespoons water

1. Trim the chicken of any fat and cut into bite-sized pieces. Put into a bowl with 2 tablespoons of the oil, the lemon zest and rosemary. Cover and marinate for at least 30 minutes or overnight in the refrigerator.

2. Heat the remaining oil in a large, heavy-bottomed frying pan with a lid. Lift the chicken pieces from the marinade, add to the pan and fry a few at a time, turning, until browned.

3. Return all the chicken to the pan. Cover and cook over a medium heat, without boiling, for about 4 minutes or until the chicken is tender. Add the cream cheese and water, season to taste with salt and pepper and reheat briefly without boiling. Serve immediately.

AUSTRALIAN RIESLING

HOME-MADE GRAVADLAX WITH
PICKLED CUCUMBER

(see page 36)

LEMON CHICKEN WITH CREAM
CHEESE AND HERBS

RHUBARB POTS

(see page 168)

Stir-fried Chicken with Mango and Coriander

SERVES 6

6 large chicken breasts, skinned and boned

2 tablespoons oil

2 red peppers, deseeded and sliced

1 × 200g/7oz tin of water chestnuts, drained

1 mango, peeled, stoned and cubed

3 spring onions, sliced on the diagonal

salt and freshly ground black pepper

FOR THE MARINADE

2.5cm/1in piece of fresh ginger root, peeled and
   chopped

2 cloves of garlic, crushed

finely grated zest of 1 orange

½ red chilli, deseeded and finely chopped

1 tablespoon ground coriander

FOR THE SAUCE

1 tablespoon cornflour

2 tablespoons light soy sauce

2 tablespoons sweet sherry

150ml/5fl oz chicken stock (see page 185)

1. Trim the chicken of any fat and cut into bite-sized pieces. Mix with all the marinade ingredients. Cover and marinate for at least 30 minutes or overnight in the refrigerator.

2. Mix together the sauce ingredients.

3. Heat the oil in a wok or large frying pan, add the chicken and cook and stir-fry for 5 minutes or until just cooked. Add the peppers and water chestnuts and stir-fry for 2 further minutes. Add the sauce mixture and bring to the boil, then reduce the heat and simmer gently for 2 minutes. Add the mango and spring onions and heat through gently. Season to taste with salt and pepper and serve immediately.

ALSACE GEWÜRZTRAMINER

PRAWN AND WATERCRESS SOUP

(see page 10)

STIR-FRIED CHICKEN WITH
MANGO AND CORIANDER

RUBY RED FRUIT PARCELS

(see page 158)

Baked Poussins with Garlic and Lemon

SERVES 6

6 × 450g/1lb one-portion poussins
6 cloves of garlic, unpeeled
6 small lemons
6 sprigs of rosemary
melted butter
salt and freshly ground black pepper
150ml/5fl oz dry white wine

TO GARNISH

1 small bunch of watercress

PRAWN SALAD WITH PINK GRAPES AND CUCUMBER

(see page 19)

BAKED POUSSINS WITH GARLIC AND LEMON

SUMMER RED FRUITS MACERATED IN ELDERFLOWER CORDIAL AND KIRSCH

(see page 164)

---

1. Preheat the oven to 200°C/400°F/gas mark 6.

2. Clean and trim the poussins. Put a clove of garlic, a whole lemon and a sprig of rosemary inside the body cavity of each poussin.

3. Tie the legs together so that the poussins are trussed and the cavity is closed. This will help to retain the shape of the birds and improve their flavour.

4. Put the poussins into a roasting dish, brush with melted butter and season with salt and pepper. Roast in the oven for 30 minutes.

5. Pour the wine evenly over the poussins and roast for 15 further minutes.

6. Remove the string from the poussins while they are still in the roasting tin. Carefully remove the garlic, lemon and rosemary from the cavity of each bird. Discard the lemons but leave the garlic and rosemary in the roasting tin.

7. Put the poussins on to a serving dish and keep warm in the turned-off oven.

8. Add a splash of cold water to the roasting tin and skim off as much fat as possible.

9. Simmer the juices in the pan for a couple of minutes. Season to taste with salt and pepper and strain into a gravy-boat.

10. Garnish the poussins with bouquets of watercress and hand the gravy separately.

AUSTRALIAN PINOT GRIGIO

Duck Breasts with Oriental Plum Sauce

SERVES 6

4 × 340g/12oz duck breasts

salt and freshly ground black pepper

4 tablespoons sesame oil

55g/2oz shallots, finely chopped

225g/8oz red plums, quartered and stoned

2.5cm/1in piece of fresh root ginger, peeled and grated

5 tablespoons light soy sauce

1 tablespoon glace de viande (see page 185) (optional)

5 tablespoons sweet sherry

1 tablespoon clear honey

1 tablespoon mustard seeds

TO GARNISH

8 spring onions

½ cucumber

SALMON RILLETTES
(see page 28)

DUCK BREASTS WITH
ORIENTAL PLUM SAUCE

A SELECTION OF CHEESES
(see page 176)

---

1. Remove the skin from the duck breasts and trim off any fat. Season with pepper.

2. Heat 1 tablespoon of the oil in a large frying pan, add the shallots and plums and sweat until soft but not coloured. Add the ginger, soy sauce, stock, sherry and honey. Bring to the boil and reduce by boiling rapidly until syrupy. Season to taste with salt and pepper and add the mustard seeds.

3. Meanwhile, prepare the garnish: cut the spring onions into 5cm/2in lengths and shred lengthwise. Soak in iced water to curl. Cut the cucumber in half, scoop out the seeds with a teaspoon and cut into thin strips lengthwise.

4. Cook the duck breasts: heat the remaining oil in a large frying pan and brown the duck on both sides. Reduce the heat and cook for 8–10 minutes, turning once. Remove from the heat and leave to stand for 5 minutes.

5. Slice the duck breasts on the diagonal and arrange on 6 individual plates. Spoon the sauce on to the plates and garnish with the drained spring onions and cucumber.

CALIFORNIAN ZINFANDEL

Glazed Duck Breasts with Apple and Sage Chutney

SERVES 6

4 × 340g/12oz duck breasts

4 teaspoons clear honey

a pinch of dry English mustard

1 teaspoon Sichuan peppercorns, lightly crushed

FOR THE CHUTNEY

2 tablespoons olive oil

1 Spanish onion, finely chopped

2 Bramley apples, peeled, cored and cut into chunks

1 teaspoon soft dark brown sugar

1 tablespoon finely chopped sage

grated zest of ¼ lemon

1 tablespoon balsamic vinegar

15g/½oz butter

salt and freshly ground black pepper

GOAT'S CHEESE WITH SESAME SEEDS AND THYME

(see page 41)

GLAZED DUCK BREASTS WITH APPLE AND SAGE CHUTNEY

PRUNE AND CHOCOLATE PUDDINGS

(see page 167)

1. Preheat the oven to 230°C/450°F/gas mark 8.

2. Remove the skin from the duck breasts and trim off any fat.

3. Mix together the honey, mustard and peppercorns and smear over the duck breasts. Set aside in the refrigerator.

4. Make the chutney: heat the oil in a large saucepan, add the onion and sweat until soft but not coloured. Add the apples, sugar, sage and lemon. Cover and cook gently until the apples are soft.

5. Add the vinegar and butter and season to taste with salt and pepper. Keep warm.

6. Meanwhile, put the duck breasts, spread side up, in a roasting tin. Season lightly with salt and pepper and roast in the oven for 12 minutes. Remove from the oven and leave to stand for 5 minutes.

7. To serve: slice the duck breasts on the diagonal. Place on 6 individual plates, pour over any pan juices and spoon a portion of apple and sage chutney beside each serving.

PREMIÈRES CÔTES DE BORDEAUX

Honey-glazed Roast Partridges

SERVES 6

6 small partridges

2 tablespoons port (optional)

salt and freshly ground black pepper

FOR THE MARINADE

4 cloves of garlic, crushed

2 tablespoons clear honey

3 tablespoons light soy sauce

2 tablespoons dark brown sugar

2 tablespoons red wine vinegar

2.5cm/1in piece of fresh root ginger, peeled and
*   finely chopped*

2 tablespoons rosemary, finely chopped

1 tablespoon Dijon mustard

2 tablespoons sesame oil

salt and freshly ground black pepper

> ⤻
>
> **CARROT CAKES WITH**
> **SPINACH SAUCE**
> *(see page 46)*
>
> **HONEY-GLAZED ROAST**
> **PARTRIDGES**
>
> **LEMON SYLLABUB**
> *(see page 170)*
>
> ⤻

TO GARNISH

1 tablespoon sesame seeds, toasted

1. Clean and trim the partridges and put into a large bowl.

2. Mix together all the marinade ingredients and pour over the partridges. Cover and leave to marinate for at least 30 minutes or overnight in the refrigerator.

3. Preheat the oven to 190°C/375°F/gas mark 5.

4. Put the partridges on a wire rack in a roasting tin. Pour in 150ml/5fl oz water. Spoon the marinade over the partridges and roast in the oven, basting occasionally, for 30 minutes.

5. Remove the partridges from the oven, put on to a serving dish and keep warm.

6. Set the roasting tin over a medium heat and reduce the juices by boiling rapidly until syrupy. Scrape the bottom of the pan to release any sediment and add water if the sauce gets too thick. Add the port, if used, and boil for a further 30 seconds. Season to taste with salt and pepper and pour over the partridges. Sprinkle with the sesame seeds and serve.

CALIFORNIAN ZINFANDEL

Venison Steaks with Cranberries and Chestnuts

SERVES 6

6 × 170g/6oz venison steaks
150ml/5fl oz beef stock (see page 184)
225g/8oz fresh cranberries
2 tablespoons redcurrant jelly
2 tablespoons port
225g/8oz chestnuts, tinned or vacuum-packed
salt and freshly ground black pepper
sugar
30g/1oz butter
1 tablespoon oil

FOR THE MARINADE

290ml/½ pint red wine
1 small onion, thickly sliced
2 bay leaves
1 strip of orange zest
6 black peppercorns
2 cloves of garlic, bruised

1. Trim the venison steaks of any membrane.

2. Mix together all the marinade ingredients and pour over the venison. Cover and leave to marinate for at least 30 minutes or overnight in the refrigerator.

3. Lift the venison from the marinade and set aside. Strain the marinade into a saucepan, add the stock and reduce by boiling rapidly until syrupy. Strain again and return to the heat. Add the cranberries and redcurrant jelly and simmer gently until the cranberries are just soft. Add the port and chestnuts and season to taste with salt, pepper and sugar if necessary. Keep warm.

4. Heat the butter and oil in a large frying pan, add the venison steaks and fry over a high heat until brown on both sides. Reduce the heat and cook for 4 further minutes on each side, depending on the thickness of the steaks.

5. Serve immediately with the warm sauce handed separately in a sauce-boat.

CHÂTEAUNEUF-DU-PAPE

SCALLOPS EN COCOTTE
(see page 32)

VENISON STEAKS
WITH CRANBERRIES
AND CHESTNUTS

A SELECTION OF CHEESES
(see page 176)

Calves' Liver with Dried Cherry Sauce

SERVES 6

675g/1½lb calves' liver, sliced
plain flour seasoned with salt and freshly ground
    black pepper
55g/2oz butter

FOR THE CHERRY SAUCE

30g/1oz butter
8 shallots, finely chopped
150g/5oz dried cherries
2 tablespoons brandy
290ml/½ pint red wine
2 tablespoons finely chopped parsley
salt and freshly ground black pepper

1. Trim the liver, removing the fine outer membrane and any large tubes.

2. Make the cherry sauce: heat the butter in a large frying pan, add the shallots and sweat until soft but not coloured. Add the cherries and brandy and heat gently. Flame the brandy and shake the pan until the flames subside. Add the wine and reduce by boiling rapidly until syrupy. Add the parsley and season to taste with salt and pepper.

3. Dip the liver in the seasoned flour and pat off any excess. Heat the butter in a large frying pan, add the liver, a few slices at a time, and fry for about 2 minutes on each side. Keep warm while frying the remaining liver in the same way.

4. To serve: place the liver on 6 individual plates, pour over the warm cherry sauce and serve immediately.

BAROLO

CHILLI SQUID SALAD
(see page 35)

CALVES' LIVER WITH DRIED
CHERRY SAUCE

LEMON CURD ICE CREAM
(see page 172)

Calves' Liver with Ginger and Pecan Sauce and Parsnip Crisps

SERVES 6

675g/1½lb calves' liver, sliced
plain flour seasoned with salt and freshly ground
    black pepper
30g/1oz unsalted butter
2 tablespoons hazelnut oil
2.5cm/1in piece of fresh root ginger, peeled and
    grated
55g/2oz pecan nuts, roughly chopped
1 tablespoon chopped thyme
1 tablespoon dark brown sugar
3 tablespoons orange juice
3 tablespoons Madeira
2 tablespoons balsamic vinegar
1 teaspoon cornflour
290ml/½ pint beef stock (see page 184)
salt and freshly ground black pepper

TO SERVE

parsnip crisps (see page 85)

1. Trim the liver, removing the fine outer membrane and any large tubes.
2. Dip the slices of liver into the seasoned flour and pat off any excess. Heat the butter and 1 tablespoon of the oil in a large frying pan until foaming. Add the liver slices, a few at a time, and fry for about 1 minute on each side until nicely browned on the outside but pale pink in the middle. Drain well and arrange in overlapping slices in an ovenproof serving dish. Keep warm while frying the remaining liver in the same way. Keep all the liver slices warm.
3. Tip off any fat in the pan. Add 2 tablespoons water, scrape up any sediment from the bottom of the pan and bring to the boil. Pour into a bowl. Taste the liquid: if it tastes burnt, substitute extra stock for it.
4. Heat the remaining oil in the pan and add the ginger, pecan nuts, thyme and sugar. Stir for 1 minute, then add the orange juice, Madeira and vinegar. Cook for 1 further minute.
5. Slake the cornflour with a little of the reserved liquid or stock and add to the pan. Add the stock gradually, then boil for at least 2 minutes until syrupy. Season with salt and pepper.
6. Pour the sauce over the liver and surround with the parsnip crisps. Serve immediately.

AUSTRALIAN PINOT NOIR

≈

MUSSEL AND SAFFRON BROTH

(see page 11)

CALVES' LIVER WITH GINGER
AND PECAN SAUCE

PRUNE AND CHOCOLATE
PUDDINGS

(see page 167)

≈

Parsnip Crisps

SERVES 6

900g/2lb parsnips
6 tablespoons hazelnut oil
extra oil

1. Peel the parsnips and, using a vegetable peeler, pare into long strips. Blanch the parsnip strips in boiling salted water for 30 seconds, then refresh under running cold water. Dry thoroughly on absorbent paper.

2. Heat the oil in a frying pan, add a few parsnip strips and fry until crisp and golden. Drain on absorbent paper and keep warm. Fry the remaining parsnip strips in batches, adding more oil as necessary.

Lambs' Kidneys with Red Onion and Sage

SERVES 6

18 lambs' kidneys

85g/3oz piece of pancetta or rindless streaky bacon

30g/1oz butter

2 large red onions, thinly sliced

3 tablespoons dry white vermouth

1 tablespoon finely chopped sage

salt and freshly ground black pepper

1. Skin the kidneys, cut them in half horizontally, remove the core with a pair of kitchen scissors and cut the kidneys into thin slices. Cut the pancetta or bacon into lardons.

2. Heat the butter in a frying pan, add the onion and sweat until soft but not coloured. Add the pancetta or bacon and fry until golden-brown. Remove from the pan with a slotted spoon and keep warm.

3. Add the kidneys to the pan and cook until brown on the outside and cooked through. Put into a sieve over a bowl to drain. Discard the juices as they can be bitter. Add the vermouth to the pan and reduce by boiling rapidly until syrupy.

4. Return the onion and bacon mixture and the kidneys to the pan, add the sage and season to taste with salt and pepper. Serve immediately.

BARBERA D'ALBA

CHICORY SALAD WITH SMOKED
OYSTERS, PECANS AND
GORGONZOLA

(see page 17)

LAMBS' KIDNEYS WITH
RED ONION AND SAGE

ROASTED COCONUT AND
RUM CREAM

(see page 175)

BEEF, LAMB AND PORK
Sauté of Beef with Beetroot and Olives

SERVES 6

675g/1½lb beef fillet
450g/1lb raw beetroot
3 tablespoons olive oil
2 tablespoons brandy
55g/2oz Kalamata black olives, pitted
2 tablespoons grainy mustard
lemon juice
salt and freshly ground black pepper
150ml/5fl oz soured cream

1. Trim the beef of any fat and sinew and cut into finger-size strips.

2. Peel the beetroot and grate coarsely.

3. Heat half the oil in a wok or large frying pan until hot but not smoking, add the beef strips, a few at a time, and stir-fry until brown but still pink in the centre. Remove from the pan and keep warm while stir-frying the remaining strips in the same way, adding more oil if necessary. When all the strips are cooked, return them to the wok or frying pan, reduce heat, add the brandy and flame, shaking the pan until the flames subside.

4. Add the beetroot and olives to the pan and stir-fry for 2 minutes or until heated through. Add the mustard and season to taste with lemon juice, salt and pepper. Pile on to a large serving dish and spoon over the soured cream.

CROZES-HERMITAGE

⌐

ALMOND AND PARSLEY SOUP
(see page 5)

SAUTÉ OF BEEF WITH BEETROOT
AND OLIVES

CITRUS FRUIT COMPOTE
WITH SPICED CARAMEL
(see page 163)

⌐

Stir-fried Beef with Sesame Paste

SERVES 6

675g/1½lb beef sirloin
3 tablespoons sesame oil
225g/8oz sugar-snap peas, topped and tailed
2 red peppers, deseeded and cut into strips
1 bunch of spring onions, sliced on the diagonal
salt and freshly ground black pepper

FOR THE SAUCE

2 tablespoons tahini
2 tablespoons light soy sauce
3 cloves of garlic, crushed
5cm/2in piece of fresh root ginger, peeled and
　　grated
2 tablespoons dry sherry
2 tablespoons clear honey
2 tablespoons Worcestershire sauce
6 tablespoons water

TO GARNISH

30g/1oz sesame seeds, toasted

1. Trim the beef of any fat and sinew and cut into finger-size strips.

2. Mix together all the sauce ingredients.

3. Heat 1 tablespoon of the oil in a wok or large frying pan until hot but not smoking, add the beef strips, a few at a time, and stir-fry until brown but still pink in the centre. Remove from the pan and keep warm while stir-frying the remaining beef in the same way, adding more oil if necessary.

4. When all the strips are cooked, reduce the heat under the wok or frying pan and add the sauce, sugar-snap peas and red pepper strips. Reduce the sauce by boiling rapidly until syrupy and the vegetables are cooked, then return the beef to the pan with the spring onions. Season to taste with salt and pepper and pile on to a large serving dish. Sprinkle over the sesame seeds and serve immediately.

RED RIOJA

BLOODY MARY CRAB SALAD

(see page 18)

**STIR-FRIED BEEF WITH
SESAME PASTE**

MARRON GLACÉ PUDDINGS

(see page 166)

Beef Stroganoff with Ginger and Chinese Five-spice

SERVES 6

675g/1½lb beef fillet

2 tablespoons oil

2 large Spanish onions, thinly sliced

2 cloves of garlic, crushed

2.5cm/1in piece of root ginger, peeled and finely chopped

2 level teaspoons Chinese five-spice powder

2 tablespoons brandy

290ml/½ pint crème fraîche

salt and freshly ground black pepper

1. Trim the beef of any fat and sinew and cut into finger-size strips.

2. Heat 1 tablespoon of the oil in a large, heavy-bottomed frying pan, add the onions and sweat until soft but not coloured. Add the garlic, ginger and five-spice powder and cook for 2–3 further minutes.

3. Remove the onion mixture from the pan and add a little of the remaining oil. Increase the heat until the oil is hot but not smoking, add the beef strips, a few at a time, and stir-fry until brown but still pink in the centre. Remove from the pan and keep warm while stir-frying the remaining strips in the same way, adding more oil if necessary. When all the strips are cooked, reduce the heat, add the brandy and flame, shaking the pan until the flames subside.

4. Return the onion mixture and beef strips to the pan and add the crème fraîche. Season to taste with salt and pepper, bring to the boil and then simmer briefly to heat the mixture through. Serve immediately.

AUSTRALIAN CABERNET SAUVIGNON

꙳

SMOKED HALIBUT PÂTÉ

(see page 27)

BEEF STROGANOFF WITH GINGER AND CHINESE FIVE-SPICE

PEAR AND MASCARPONE PUFFS

(see page 152)

꙳

Fillet Steaks with Parsnip and Sesame Cakes

Serves 6

6 × 170g/6oz fillet steaks

2 tablespoons sesame oil

1 medium onion, finely chopped

4 medium parsnips, peeled and grated

2 tablespoons crème fraîche or double cream

2 tablespoons sesame seeds, toasted

1 tablespoon snipped chives

salt and freshly ground black pepper

1. Trim the fillet steaks of any fat and sinew.

2. Preheat the oven to 200°C/400°F/gas mark 6.

3. Heat 1 tablespoon of the oil in a large frying pan, add the onion and sweat until soft but not coloured. Add the parsnips and cook for 4–5 minutes until opaque.

4. Stir in the crème fraîche or cream, sesame seeds and chives and season to taste with salt and pepper. Divide the mixture between 12 lightly greased patty tins.

5. Bake in the oven for about 15 minutes or until golden-brown.

6. Meanwhile, heat the remaining oil in a large frying pan, add the steaks and cook over a high heat for 5–8 minutes, depending on thickness, until brown on the outside and pink in the centre.

7. To serve: place a steak and 2 parsnip cakes on each of 6 individual plates and serve immediately.

VOSNE-ROMANÉE

⌣

CEVICHE

(see page 34)

FILLET STEAKS WITH PARSNIP
AND SESAME CAKES

CHESTNUT PUDDINGS

(see page 155)

⌣

Tournedos with Wild Mushrooms and Truffle Mash

SERVES 6

6 × 170g/6oz tournedos
salt and freshly ground black pepper

FOR THE TRUFFLE MASH

900g/2lb potatoes, peeled
150ml/5fl oz milk
1 clove of garlic
1 sprig of thyme
5 tablespoons olive oil
1 truffle, finely diced
1 teaspoon truffle oil
1 tablespoon finely chopped parsley

3 tablespoons olive oil
6 shallots, finely chopped
2 cloves of garlic, crushed
250g/9oz wild mushrooms, picked over
340/12oz field mushrooms, sliced
3 sprigs of thyme

**CHICORY SALAD WITH
SMOKED OYSTERS, PECANS
AND GORGONZOLA**

(see page 17)

**TOURNEDOS WITH
WILD MUSHROOMS AND
TRUFFLE MASH**

HONEY AND FIG CUSTARDS

(see page 157)

---

5 tablespoons dry white wine
2 tablespoons brandy
150ml/5fl oz beef stock (see page 184)
½ teaspoon tomato purée

1. Make the truffle mash: cook the potatoes in boiling salted water for 15–20 minutes or until soft. Drain thoroughly and return to the pan to dry out.

2. Meanwhile, heat the milk with the garlic and thyme and infuse for 10 minutes. Push the potatoes through a mouli or sieve and strain in the hot milk. Mix thoroughly and add the oil, truffle, truffle oil and parsley. Season to taste with salt and pepper, mix well and set aside.

3. Make the mushroom mixture: heat 2 tablespoons of the olive oil in a large frying pan, add the shallots and garlic and sweat until soft but not coloured. Add the mushrooms and thyme and continue to cook until soft. Add the wine and reduce by boiling rapidly until syrupy. Season to taste with salt and pepper and set aside.

4. Season the steaks with salt and pepper and rub with the remaining oil. Heat a large frying pan until very hot, add the steaks and fry until cooked to taste. Remove from the pan and keep warm.
5. Add the brandy to the pan and flame. When the flames have subsided, add the stock and tomato purée and reduce by boiling rapidly until syrupy. Season to taste with salt and pepper. Reheat the mash and the mushrooms and serve immediately with the steaks and pan sauce.

SAINT-JULIEN

Veal Martini

SERVES 6

6 × 170g/6oz veal escalopes
salt and freshly ground black pepper
30g/1oz unsalted butter
1 tablespoon finely chopped sage
3 tablespoons dry white vermouth
6 tablespoons double cream

TO GARNISH

watercress

1. Trim the veal carefully and season with salt and pepper.
2. Heat the butter in a large frying pan until foaming and just turning brown. Add the veal, in batches if necessary, and fry for about 1 minute on each side until lightly browned and just cooked. Do not overcook. Remove the escalopes from the pan and keep warm in a serving dish.
3. Tip off all the fat from the pan. Wipe out the pan if at all burnt. Add 4 tablespoons water, the sage and vermouth. Bring to the boil and reduce by boiling rapidly to half the original quality.
4. Scrape any sediment from the bottom of the pan. Add the cream and bring to the boil, then reduce the heat and simmer until thickened slightly. Season to taste with salt and pepper and pour over the veal. Garnish with bouquets of watercress and serve immediately.

WHITE GRAVES

~

CARROT AND CUMIN SOUP

(see page 6)

VEAL MARTINI

SUMMER RED FRUITS
MACERATED IN ELDERFLOWER
CORDIAL AND KIRSCH

(see page 164)

~

Lamb Cutlets with Sun-dried Tomato and Chilli Couscous

SERVES 6

3 × 6-cutlet racks of lamb, trimmed
salt and freshly ground black pepper
2 tablespoons olive oil

FOR THE COUSCOUS

290ml/½ pint water
150ml/5fl oz tomato juice
1 tablespoon chilli sauce
1 clove of garlic, crushed
2 tablespoons lemon juice
2 teaspoons clear honey
225g/8oz couscous
55g/2oz sundried tomatoes, sliced
1 tablespoon chopped mint

1. Preheat the oven to 240°C/475°F/gas mark 8.
2. Trim the lamb cutlets of any excess fat and season lightly with salt and pepper. Put into a roasting tin and drizzle over the olive oil.
3. Roast the lamb in the oven for 15-20 minutes or until still pink in the centre. Remove from the oven and leave to stand for 5 minutes.
4. Meanwhile, prepare the couscous: bring the water and tomato juice to the boil in a saucepan and add the chilli sauce, garlic, lemon juice and honey. Simmer for 2–3 minutes, then pour over the couscous. Add the sundried tomatoes, season to taste with salt and pepper and leave to stand for 5 minutes.
5. To serve: stir the mint into the couscous and pile on to 6 individual plates. Carve the lamb and arrange 3 cutlets on each plate. Serve immediately.

AUSTRALIAN SHIRAZ

ROAST AUBERGINE DIP
(see page 23)

ROAST GARLIC DIP
(see page 24)

OLIVE AND CHILLI DIP
(see page 25)

LAMB CUTLETS WITH SUN-DRIED TOMATO AND CHILLI COUSCOUS

APPLES WITH CARAMELIZED CRESCENTS
(see page 160)

Lamb Cutlets with a Cornmeal Crust and Tomato and Mint Salsa

SERVES 6

18 lamb cutlets
salt and freshly ground black pepper
2 eggs, beaten
110g/4oz fine cornmeal or polenta
55g/2oz dry white breadcrumbs
85g/3oz butter, melted
1 tablespoon chopped oregano
grated zest of 1 lemon

TO SERVE

1 quantity tomato and mint salsa (see page 195)

1. Trim the lamb cutlets of any excess fat and season with salt and pepper.

2. Dip the cutlets in the beaten eggs.

3. Mix together all the remaining ingredients and season to taste with salt and pepper. Roll the lamb cutlets in the mixture, patting off any excess. Put on a greased baking sheet and chill thoroughly.

4. Preheat the grill to its highest setting.

5. Grill the cutlets for 3–4 minutes on each side.

6. To serve: place 3 cutlets on each of 6 individual plates and serve immediately with the tomato and mint salsa handed separately.

MONTEPULCIANO D'ABRUZZO

SPRING VEGETABLES IN
THAI-STYLE DRESSING

(see page 45)

LAMB CUTLETS WITH A
CORNMEAL CRUST AND TOMATO
AND MINT SALSA

LEMON CURD ICE CREAM

(see page 172)

Fillet of Lamb with Soy Sauce, Ginger and Garlic

Lamb neck fillet is quite fatty, so do not try to remove all the fat. It bastes the meat as it cooks and makes it very succulent.

SERVES 6

3 × 340g/12oz lamb fillets

4 tablespoons light soy sauce

3 tablespoons rice wine vinegar

1½ tablespoons sesame oil

2 cloves of garlic, bruised

2.5cm/1in piece of fresh root ginger, peeled and roughly chopped

lemon juice

salt and freshly ground black pepper

1. Trim the lamb, removing any large pieces of fat or gristle.

2. Mix together all the remaining ingredients and pour over the lamb fillets. Marinate for at least 30 minutes or overnight in the refrigerator.

3. Preheat the oven to 240°C/475°F/gas mark 8.

4. Heat a large, heavy-bottomed frying pan with no oil in it, until it is very hot. Lift the lamb fillets from the marinade and add them to the pan. Take care as they may spit. Fry the fillets quickly on all sides until they have a dark brown crust.

5. Put the fillets into a roasting tin and roast in the oven for 8–10 minutes until cooked but still pink in the centre. Remove from the oven and leave to stand for 5 minutes.

6. Meanwhile, put the marinade into a small saucepan and reduce by boiling rapidly until syrupy. Taste and season with more lemon juice, salt and pepper if necessary.

7. To serve: slice the lamb fillets on the diagonal and place on 6 individual plates. Strain over the reduced marinade and serve immediately.

CALIFORNIAN ZINFANDEL

> ↬
>
> **MUSHROOMS WITH ARTICHOKE HEARTS AND OLIVES**
> *(see page 50)*
>
> **FILLET OF LAMB WITH SOY SAUCE, GINGER AND GARLIC**
>
> **LEMON SYLLABUB**
> *(see page 170)*
>
> ↬

Rack of Lamb with Mustard and Breadcrumbs

SERVES 6

3 × 6-cutlet racks of lamb, trimmed

6 teaspoons pale French mustard

3 tablespoons fresh white breadcrumbs

3 tablespoons chopped fresh herbs (mint, chives,
    parsley and thyme)

½ teaspoon salt

½ teaspoon freshly ground black pepper

55g/2oz unsalted butter

1. Preheat the oven to 220°C/425°F/gas mark 7.

2. Trim off as much fat as possible from the meat.

3. Mix together the mustard, breadcrumbs, herbs, salt, pepper and butter. Press a thin layer of this mixture over the rounded, skinned side of the racks.

4. Place them, crumbed side up, in a roasting tin and roast for 20–25 minutes. This will give pink, slightly underdone lamb. Allow to rest in a warm place for 5 minutes. Serve with the butter and juices from the pan poured over the top.

AUSTRALIAN CABERNET SAUVIGNON

CHILLI SQUID SALAD

(see page 35)

RACK OF LAMB WITH MUSTARD
AND BREADCRUMBS

A SELECTION OF CHEESES

(see page 176)

Collops of Lamb with Flageolet Beans and Oyster Mushrooms

SERVES 6

3 × 340g/12oz lamb fillets

5 tablespoons chopped sage

3 cloves of garlic, bruised

salt and freshly ground black pepper

2 tablespoons good-quality olive oil

30g/1oz butter

340g/12oz oyster mushrooms, torn into strips

2 × 450g/14oz tins of flageolet beans, drained and rinsed

2 tablespoons cider vinegar

1. Trim the lamb of any large pieces of fat or gristle. Rub the meat with 2 tablespoons of the sage and the garlic and season with pepper. Drizzle with the oil and marinate for at least 30 minutes or overnight in the refrigerator.

2. Preheat the oven to 240°C/475°F/gas mark 8.

3. Heat a large, heavy-bottomed frying pan with no oil in it until it is very hot. Lift the lamb fillets from the marinade and add them to the pan. Take care as they may split. Fry quickly until brown on all sides.

4. Put the fillets into a roasting tin and roast in the oven for 8–10 minutes until the lamb is cooked but still pink in the centre. Allow to rest in a warm place for 5 minutes.

5. Meanwhile, melt the butter in a large frying pan, add the oyster mushrooms and cook for 2–3 minutes or until soft. Add the flageolet beans and the remaining sage and heat through. Add the cider vinegar and season to taste with salt and pepper. Keep warm.

6. To serve: slice the lamb fillets on the diagonal, place on 6 individual plates and serve with the sauce handed separately.

CHIANTI CLASSICO

SMOKED HALIBUT WITH
JAPANESE-STYLE CUCUMBER
SALAD
(see page 39)

COLLOPS OF LAMB WITH
FLAGEOLET BEANS AND
OYSTER MUSHROOMS

CHOCOLATE BREAD AND
BUTTER PUDDING
(see page 153)

Noisettes of Lamb with Apricot and Caper Jam

SERVES 6

12 × 85g/3oz lamb noisettes

olive oil

salt and freshly ground black pepper

FOR THE APRICOT AND CAPER JAM

1 tablespoon olive oil

1 Spanish onion, sliced

5 tablespoons dry white wine

225g/8oz no-need-to-soak dried apricots, roughly chopped

1 tablespoon mustard seeds

½ tablespoon finely chopped rosemary

a pinch of cayenne pepper

1 tablespoon cider vinegar

2 tablespoons capers, rinsed and drained

salt and freshly ground black pepper

1. Make the apricot and caper jam: heat the oil in a large saucepan, add the onion and sweat over a low heat until soft but not coloured. Add the wine and reduce by boiling rapidly to half its original quantity. Add the apricots, mustard seeds, rosemary and cayenne and cook until the apricots are soft and the liquid syrupy. Add the vinegar and capers and season to taste with salt and pepper.

2. Preheat the grill to its highest setting. Drizzle a little oil on the lamb noisettes and season lightly with salt and pepper. Grill for 5 minutes on each side (the meat should be slightly pink in the centre). Serve immediately with a spoonful of warm apricot and caper jam on each plate.

GIGONDAS

MUSHROOMS WITH ARTICHOKE
HEARTS AND OLIVES
(see page 50)

NOISETTES OF LAMB WITH
APRICOT AND CAPER JAM

A SELECTION OF CHEESES
(see page 176)

Pork Medallions with Butter Bean Mash

SERVES 6

3 × 340g/12oz pork fillets

2 tablespoons oil

FOR THE MARINADE

150ml/5fl oz olive oil

finely grated zest of 1 lemon

1 sprig of thyme, finely chopped

freshly ground black pepper

FOR THE BUTTER BEAN MASH

190ml/6½fl oz water

3 cloves of garlic, peeled

*2 × 400g/14oz tins of butter beans, drained and
  rinsed*

finely grated zest and juice of 1 lemon

salt and freshly ground black pepper

1 tablespoon chopped thyme

↩

SCALLOPS EN COCOTTE

(see page 32)

PORK MEDALLIONS WITH
BUTTER BEAN MASH

SUMMER RED FRUITS
MACERATED IN ELDERFLOWER
CORDIAL AND KIRSCH

(see page 164)

↩

TO SERVE

1 quantity coriander pesto (see page 31)

1. Trim the pork fillets and cut each into 6 medallions.

2. Mix together all the marinade ingredients and pour over the pork medallions. Cover and leave to marinate for at least 30 minutes or overnight in the refrigerator.

3. Make the butter bean mash: put the water and garlic into a saucepan, bring to the boil and add the butter beans. Reduce the heat and simmer until the beans are falling apart and the garlic is soft. Sieve the mixture and return to the rinsed-out pan. Add the zest and lemon juice and season to taste with salt and pepper. Add the thyme.

4. Lift the pork from the marinade and drain well. Season with salt and pepper.

5. Heat the oil in a large frying pan, add the medallions, a few at a time, and fry until they are golden-brown and just cooked.

6. To serve: put 3 medallions on each of 6 individual plates with a portion of the butter bean mash and a spoonful of coriander pesto beside each serving.

VOLNAY

Pork Medallions with Yellow Pepper Relish

SERVES 6
3 × 340g/12oz pork fillets
1 tablespoon oil
4 tablespoons medium cider
salt and freshly ground black pepper
½ tablespoon dark brown sugar

FOR THE MARINADE
6 tablespoons olive oil
1 tablespoon cider vinegar
2 dried red chillies, split in half
2 sprigs of fresh rosemary
10 black peppercorns

FOR THE RELISH
2 tablespoons cider vinegar
30g/1oz raisins
4 yellow peppers
6 tablespoons olive oil
2 shallots, chopped
½ tablespoon olive oil
1 tablespoon mustard seeds, dry-roasted
½ teaspoon cayenne pepper (optional)
salt and freshly ground black pepper

CEVICHE

(see page 34)

PORK MEDALLIONS WITH
YELLOW PEPPER RELISH

GLAZED FRUITS AND CHESTNUTS
IN MADEIRA SYRUP

(see page 159)

1. Trim the pork fillets.

2. Whisk together all the marinade ingredients and pour over the pork fillets. Cover and marinate for at least 30 minutes or overnight in the refrigerator.

3. Make the relish: pour the vinegar over the raisins and set aside.

4. Preheat the grill to its highest setting. Cut the peppers into quarters and remove the stalks, inner membrane and seeds. Grill the peppers, skin side uppermost, until the skins are black and blistered. Using a small knife, scrape off the skin. Cut into 2.5cm/1in diagonal pieces.

5. Heat the oil in a frying pan. Add the shallots and sweat until soft but not coloured. Add the yellow peppers, raisins and vinegar, mustard seeds and cayenne pepper, if used. Simmer, stirring, for a few minutes, adding a little water if necessary. Taste and season well with salt and pepper.

6. Preheat the oven to 180°C/350°F/gas mark 4.
7. Lift the pork fillets from the marinade. Heat the oil in a large frying pan, add the fillets and fry quickly until browned on all sides. Put them into a casserole and pour in the cider. Season with salt and pepper. Cover and cook in the oven for 20 minutes or until tender.
8. Allow to rest for 5 minutes in a warm place. Slice the cooked pork into medallions and arrange on a serving dish. Reheat the relish and pour over the pork. Keep warm.
9. Strain the cooking juices into a saucepan, add the sugar, and reduce by boiling rapidly until syrupy. Hand separately with the pork.

AUSTRALIAN CHARDONNAY SEMILLON

Pork Noisettes with Pumpkin and Cherry Tomato Chutney

Pork noisettes are appearing in some supermarkets, but it is easy to make your own if you have the time. Remove the skin and bone from a loin pork chop, wrap the fat around the eye of the meat and tie up with string.

SERVES 6

6 × 225g/8oz pork noisettes
1 tablespoon finely chopped thyme
salt and freshly ground black pepper

FOR THE CHUTNEY

2 tablespoons olive oil
1 large Spanish onion, thinly sliced
570g/1¼lb pumpkin or butternut squash, peeled, seeded and cut into chunks
2 cloves of garlic, crushed
2 sprigs of thyme
½ teaspoon ground cumin
1 teaspoon light brown sugar

GRILLED TIGER PRAWNS WITH
CORIANDER PESTO

(see page 31)

PORK NOISETTES WITH PUMPKIN
AND CHERRY TOMATO CHUTNEY

PRUNE AND CHOCOLATE
PUDDINGS

(see page 167)

salt and freshly ground black pepper
225g/8oz cherry tomatoes
1 tablespoon balsamic vinegar
2 tablespoons pumpkin seeds, dry-roasted (optional)

1. Trim the pork noisettes and sprinkle with the thyme.

2. Preheat the grill to its highest setting.

3. Start the chutney: heat the oil in a large frying pan with a lid, add the onion and sweat until soft but not coloured. Add the pumpkin, garlic, thyme, cumin and sugar. Season to taste with salt and pepper, cover and cook for 5 minutes or until the pumpkin is beginning to soften. Remove the lid and cook for 10 further minutes or until the pumpkin is soft and beginning to brown.

4. Season the pork noisettes with salt and pepper and grill for 6–8 minutes on each side or until cooked.

5. Add the cherry tomatoes to the chutney with the vinegar and heat through gently. The mixture should not be runny. If it is, simmer gently to reduce. Remove and discard the sprigs of thyme and add the pumpkin seeds.

6. To serve: put a pork noisette on to each of 6 individual plates and spoon a portion of the pumpkin and cherry tomato chutney beside each serving. Serve immediately.

CÔTES DE VENTOUX

Pork Fillet with Saffron Bread Sauce and Pan-fried Pears

SERVES 6

3 × 340g/12oz pork fillets
1 tablespoon oil
salt and freshly ground black pepper
290ml/½ pint apple juice
290ml/½ pint chicken stock
30g/1oz unsalted butter
2 large ripe pears, peeled, cored and quartered
salt and freshly ground black pepper
2 teaspoons arrowroot

FOR THE SAFFRON BREAD SAUCE

290ml/½ pint milk
1 small onion, thickly sliced
1 bay leaf
¼ teaspoon saffron strands
55g/2oz fresh white breadcrumbs
30g/1oz ground almonds
55g/2oz butter

~

SALMON RILLETTES

(see page 28)

PORK FILLET WITH SAFFRON BREAD SAUCE AND PAN-FRIED PEARS

ALAIN SENDERENS' SOUPE AUX FRUITS EXOTIQUES

(see page 173)

~

---

1. Preheat the oven to 200°C/400°F/gas mark 6.

2 Trim the pork fillets. Heat the oil in a large frying pan, add the pork fillets and fry until golden-brown on all sides. Season with salt and pepper and put into a shallow flameproof casserole with the apple juice and stock. Cover and cook in the oven for about 30 minutes or until cooked.

3. Meanwhile, make the saffron bread sauce: heat the milk with the onion, bay leaf and saffron and simmer gently for 5 minutes. Remove the onion and bay leaf, being careful to retain the saffron strands. Pour the milk over the breadcrumbs and ground almonds in a bowl. Return the mixture to the rinsed-out pan and heat through gently. Add the butter and season to taste with salt and pepper. Keep warm.

4. Heat the butter in a large frying pan until foaming. Add the pears and fry until golden-brown. Remove and keep warm.

5. Lift the pork from the cooking juices and set aside. Taste the juices and reduce by boiling if necessary, mix the arrowroot with a little of the hot sauce and return to the pan. Bring to the boil, season to taste with salt and pepper.

6. To serve: slice the pork fillet on the diagonal, arrange on a large serving dish and strain over the reduced cooking juices. Arrange the pears on the dish with the pork and serve with the saffron bread sauce handed separately.

FLEURIE

MAIN-COURSE SALADS
Lobster Salad

Cooked lobster tails can often be bought in supermarkets and fishmongers. If you have trouble obtaining them, buy whole lobsters and use the claws as a garnish.

SERVES 6

6 large cooked lobster tails

2 large ripe mangoes

2 large ripe avocados

4 oranges

FOR THE DRESSING

250g/8oz mascarpone cheese

290ml/½ pint single cream

1 tablespoon sherry vinegar

2 tablespoons tomato purée

salt and freshly ground black pepper

8 tomatoes, peeled, deseeded and cut into strips

↩

GOAT'S CHEESE WITH SESAME
SEEDS AND THYME
(see page 51)

LOBSTER SALAD

LEMON AND RASPBERRY
CRÈMES
(see page 156)

↩

TO SERVE

1 head of frisée lettuce

1. Remove the lobster meat from the shell and cut into medallions 1cm/½in thick.

2. Peel and stone the mangoes and avocados and cut the flesh into 2cm/1in chunks. Peel and segment the oranges. Add the mangoes, avocados and orange segments to the lobster meat.

3. Make the dressing: mix together the mascarpone, cream, vinegar and tomato purée. Season to taste with salt and pepper and gently stir in the tomato strips, reserving a few to garnish.

4. Put a small handful of frisée leaves on to each of 6 individual plates and pile on the lobster mixture. Pour over the dressing and garnish with the reserved tomato.

CHABLIS PREMIER CRU

Grilled Cured Salmon Salad with Horseradish Dressing

SERVES 6

900g/2lb salmon fillet, skinned
170g/6oz sea salt
170g/6oz caster sugar
15g/½oz freshly ground white pepper
1 bunch of dill, chopped
oil for brushing

FOR THE SALAD

radicchio
lamb's lettuce
rocket
225g/8oz mangetout, topped and tailed

FOR THE DRESSING

4 tablespoons sunflower oil
1 tablespoon lemon juice
½ tablespoon fresh grated horseradish
salt and freshly ground black pepper

MUSHROOMS WITH ARTICHOKE
HEARTS AND OLIVES

(see page 50)

GRILLED CURED SALMON SALAD
WITH HORSERADISH DRESSING

CITRUS FRUIT COMPOTE WITH
SPICED CARAMEL

(see page 163)

TO GARNISH

2 tablespoons snipped chives

1. Trim the salmon fillet and remove any bones.

2. Mix together the salt, sugar, pepper and dill and spread half the mixture in a dish large enough to take the salmon. Put the fish on top and spread over the remaining salt mixture. Cover tightly and refrigerate for 12 hours or overnight.

3. Wash the salmon thoroughly and pat dry with absorbent paper. Slice the fish, on the diagonal, into strips 5mm/¼in thick.

4. Preheat the grill to its highest setting.

5. Blanch the mangetout in boiling salted water and refresh under running cold water. Add to the salad leaves and mix together.

6. Mix together all the dressing ingredients, seasoning to taste with salt and pepper.

7. Toss the salad leaves thoroughly with the dressing and divide between 6 individual plates.

8. Put the salmon slices on to a lightly oiled baking sheet and grill very quickly on one side only so that the fish is barely cooked. Arrange the salmon on the salad leaves and serve immediately.

WHITE SANCERRE

Monkfish Salad with Green Sauce

SERVES 6

1.35kg/3lb monkfish fillet, skinned

FOR THE MARINADE

finely grated zest and juice of 2 limes
4 tablespoons olive oil
freshly ground black pepper

FOR THE GREEN SAUCE

85g/3oz coriander, stems and leaves
85g/3oz creamed coconut
½ green chilli, deseeded and finely chopped
½ teaspoon Chinese five-spice powder
salt and freshly ground black pepper
5 tablespoons water

TO SERVE

2 tablespoons oil
*1 small green pepper, deseeded and roughly
    chopped*
225g/8oz sugar-snap peas, topped and tailed

SWEET AND SPICY AUBERGINE
KEBABS

(see page 44)

MONKFISH SALAD WITH
GREEN SAUCE

GINGER SYLLABUB

(see page 171)

---

1. Trim the monkfish of any membrane and brown flesh. Cut into large chunks.

2. Mix together all the marinade ingredients and pour over the monkfish. Cover and marinate for at least 30 minutes or overnight in the refrigerator.

3. Make the green sauce: put all the ingredients into a food processor, reserving a few sprigs of coriander for garnish, and process until smooth. Season to taste with salt and pepper.

4. Lift the monkfish from the marinade.

5. Heat the oil in a large frying pan, add the monkfish and cook over a medium heat for 6 minutes, turning once. With a slotted spoon, remove the fish into a large bowl. Add the marinade to the pan with the green pepper and sugar-snap peas. Bring to the boil and cook until the vegetables are soft and the marinade has thickened. Add the green sauce and season to taste with salt and pepper.

6. Pour the mixture over the monkfish, stir carefully and leave to get completely cold.

7. To serve: pile into a large serving dish and garnish with the reserved coriander leaves.

WHITE RIOJA

Warm Chicken Salad

This salad can be adapted according to what salad ingredients there are in your refrigerator. It can easily be made into a complete meal with the addition of hot new potatoes. The essential ingredients (other than the chicken!) are the rocket, chives, walnut oil and balsamic vinegar. It is also very good made with breast of pheasant instead of the chicken.

SERVES 6

6 chicken breasts, skinned and boned
plain flour seasoned with salt and freshly ground
   black pepper
salad leaves, such as frisée, lamb's lettuce, gem
   lettuce, rocket
170g/6oz baby sweetcorn
170g/6oz broccoli
salt and freshly ground black pepper
3 tablespoons sunflower oil
170g/6oz shiitake or chestnut mushrooms
1 bunch of chives, chopped
6 tablespoons walnut oil
2 tablespoons balsamic vinegar

1. Remove any fat from the chicken breasts, cut into bite-sized pieces and coat them lightly with the seasoned flour. Put them on to a plate, making sure that they are not touching.

2. Put the salad leaves into a large salad bowl.

3.. Cook the sweetcorn and broccoli in a small amount of boiling salted water.

4. Meanwhile, heat 2 tablespoons of the oil in a large frying pan, add the chicken and fry for about 5 minutes until browned on all sides. Reduce the heat and continue to fry until the chicken is nearly cooked. Fry the mushrooms in the remaining oil in a second pan.

5. Drain the broccoli and sweetcorn. Drain the chicken pieces on absorbent paper.

6. Transfer all the ingredients to the salad bowl, mix together, season well with salt and pepper and serve immediately.

CALIFORNIAN SAUVIGNON BLANC

∽

THREE-CHEESE PÂTÉ
WITH PECANS
(see page 26)

WARM CHICKEN SALAD

RUBY RED FRUIT PARCELS
(see page 158)

∽

FILLET STEAKS WITH PARSNIP AND SESAME CAKES

NOISETTES OF LAMB WITH APRICOT AND CAPER JAM

PORK FILLET WITH SAFFRON BREAD SAUCE AND PAN-FRIED PEARS

WARM PIGEON BREAST AND CRACKED WHEAT SALAD

THREE PEA PASTA

PEAR AND MASCARPONE PUFFS

CHOCOLATE RUM AND RAISIN PUDDINGS

CITRUS FRUIT COMPOTE WITH SPICED CARAMEL

Smoked Chicken and Noodle Salad

SERVES 6

1 smoked chicken

225g/8oz egg noodles

3 tablespoons oil

110g/4oz rindless streaky bacon, cut into strips

2 cloves of garlic, crushed

2 parsnips, peeled and grated

110g/4oz mangetout, topped and tailed

FOR THE DRESSING

2 tablespoons sesame oil

2 tablespoons light soy sauce

2 tablespoons balsamic vinegar

1 tablespoon clear honey

a pinch of cayenne pepper

1cm/½in piece of fresh root ginger, peeled and grated

finely grated zest of ½ lemon

salt and freshly ground black pepper

TO GARNISH

1 tablespoon sesame seeds, toasted

1. Skin and bone the chicken and pull the meat into bite-sized pieces.

2. Bring a large saucepan of salted water to the boil, add the noodles and immediately remove from the heat. Leave to stand for 6 minutes, then drain, refresh under running cold water and place in a large bowl.

3. Heat the oil in a large frying pan, add the bacon and fry until brown. Add the garlic and parsnips and cook until very soft. Add the mangetout and cook for 2 further minutes, or until the mangetout have just wilted. Remove from the heat and allow to cool.

4. Mix together all the dressing ingredients and pour over the noodles. Add the chicken, bacon, parsnips and mangetout and mix thoroughly. Season to taste with salt and pepper.

5. To serve: pile into a serving bowl and sprinkle with the sesame seeds.

BARBERA D'ASTI

PRAWN AND WATERCRESS SOUP

(see page 10)

SMOKED CHICKEN AND NOODLE SALAD

FIGS WITH GOAT'S CHEESE AND PECAN CARAMEL

(see page 162)

Thai Duck Salad

SERVES 6

4 large duck breasts, skinned

1 tablespoon Chinese five-spice powder

1 teaspoon Sichuan peppercorns, roasted and crushed

450g/1lb sugar-snap peas, topped and tailed

FOR THE MARINADE

3 tablespoons sesame oil

2 small onions, finely chopped

5 tablespoons dry sherry

5 tablespoons light soy sauce

1 stick of lemon grass, finely chopped

½ green chilli, deseeded and finely chopped

FOR THE DRESSING

juice of 1 lime

4 tablespoons oil

1 tablespoon finely chopped coriander

salt and freshly ground black pepper

❧

INDIVIDUAL ARNOLD BENNETT SOUFFLÉS

(see page 43)

THAI DUCK SALAD

FRIED PEARS WITH MACADAMIAS AND PINENUTS

(see page 161)

❧

---

1. Trim the duck breasts carefully and rub the spices into the flesh.

2. Mix together all the marinade ingredients, pour over the duck breasts and leave to marinate for at least 30 minutes or overnight in the refrigerator.

3. Preheat the oven to 230°C/450°F/gas mark 8.

4. Lift the duck breasts from the marinade. Put them into a roasting tin and roast in the oven for 10–12 minutes.

5. Meanwhile, pour the marinade into a saucepan. Bring to the boil and boil until the onions are softened and the liquid has reduced to 2 tablespoons. Remove from the heat and set aside.

6. Meanwhile, blanch the sugar-snap peas in boiling salted water and refresh under running cold water.

7. Mix together all the dressing ingredients in a large bowl, seasoning to taste with salt and pepper, and pour over the sugar-snap peas, mixing thoroughly.

8. Remove the duck from the oven and leave to stand for 5 minutes. Strain the cooking juices into the reduced marinade. Reduce again by boiling rapidly to 2 tablespoons.

9. Slice the duck breasts on the diagonal and mix together with the sugar-snap peas and cooled sauce. Pile into a serving bowl and serve immediately.

BEAUJOLAIS

Brown Rice Salad with Duck

SERVES 6

310g/11oz brown rice

3 duck breasts, skinned

½ teaspoon mixed ground cumin and coriander

3 tablespoons pumpkin seeds, toasted

110g/4oz seedless pink grapes

2 tablespoons snipped chives

FOR THE DRESSING

2 tablespoons olive oil

3 tablespoons walnut oil

1 tablespoon sunflower oil

1 onion, finely chopped

1 tablespoon red wine vinegar

1 teaspoon Dijon mustard

4 anchovy fillets, drained and mashed

salt and freshly ground black pepper

Tabasco sauce

CEVICHE

(see page 34)

BROWN RICE SALAD
WITH DUCK

ROASTED COCONUT AND
RUM CREAM

(see page 175)

TO SERVE

radicchio

2 spring onions, sliced

1. Preheat the oven to 230°C/450°F/gas mark 8.

2. Cook the rice in a large saucepan of boiling salted water for about 30–40 minutes or until cooked. Refresh under running cold water, drain and dry thoroughly on absorbent paper.

3. Remove any fat from the duck breasts and rub the cumin and coriander into the flesh.

4. Put them in a roasting tin and roast in the oven for 10–12 minutes. Remove from the oven and allow to cool.

5. Meanwhile, make the dressing: heat the oils in a frying pan, add the onion and sweat until soft but not coloured. Mix with all the remaining dressing ingredients in a large bowl, season to taste with salt, pepper and Tabasco sauce, if used.

6. Cut the duck breasts into bite-size pieces and stir into the dressing with the rice, pumpkin seeds, grapes and chives. Season to taste with salt, pepper and more Tabasco, if used.

7. To serve: arrange the radicchio leaves on 6 individual plates. Pile on the salad and sprinkle with the spring onions. Serve immediately.

ALSACE RIESLING

Smoked Duck and Baby Corn Salad

This recipe is equally successful using smoked ham, chicken or venison. If you cannot find Japanese Teriake marinade, use equal quantities of medium sherry and soy sauce instead.

SERVES 6

30g/1oz butter

225g/8oz baby corn

2 red peppers, deseeded and cut into slivers

2 tablespoons Teriake marinade

110g/4oz sun-dried tomatoes in oil, drained and sliced

500g/1¼lb smoked duck, sliced

2 tablespoons sunflower seeds, toasted

FOR THE DRESSING

3 tablespoons sunflower oil

1 tablespoon red wine vinegar

1 teaspoon Dijon mustard

salt and freshly ground black pepper

TO SERVE

1 head of frisée lettuce

110g/4oz Gruyère cheese, coarsely grated

1. Melt the butter in a large frying pan, add the baby corn and cook until golden-brown. Add the red peppers and cook until soft. Add the Teriake marinade and cook for 30 seconds, then add the sun-dried tomatoes, smoked duck and sunflower seeds.

2. Meanwhile, mix together all the dressing ingredients, seasoning to taste with salt and pepper, and toss with the frisée lettuce.

3. To serve: arrange the leaves on a large serving dish, pile on the duck mixture and sprinkle with the cheese. Serve immediately.

BEAUJOLAIS

↵

THREE-CHEESE PÂTÉ
WITH PECANS

(see page 26)

SMOKED DUCK AND BABY
CORN SALAD

BAKED BANANAS IN
AMARETTI CRUMBLE

(see page 151)

↵

Warm Pigeon Breast and Cracked Wheat Salad

For this recipe chicken or duck can be used to replace the pigeon.

SERVES 6

12 pigeon breasts, skinned
170g/6oz cracked wheat or bulghar
3 tablespoons sesame oil
½ red chilli, deseeded and finely chopped
*2.5cm/1in piece of fresh root ginger, peeled and
   grated*
110g/4oz shiitake mushrooms, sliced
110g/4oz Parma ham, sliced
140g/5oz plum jam
5 spring onions, sliced on the diagonal
*55g/2oz sun-dried tomatoes in oil, drained and
   sliced*
salt and freshly ground black pepper
lemon juice
30g/1oz pinenuts, toasted
½ cucumber, deseeded and finely chopped
2 tablespoons oil

FOR THE MARINADE

1 tablespoon Chinese five-spice powder
1 tablespoon light soy sauce

TO GARNISH

2 tablespoons snipped chives

1. Mix together the marinade ingredients and coat the pigeon breasts on both sides. Put into a shallow dish, cover and leave to marinate for at least 30 minutes or overnight in the refrigerator.

2. Put the cracked wheat or bulghar into a bowl and cover with cold water. Leave to stand for 15 minutes. Drain thoroughly, squeeze out any remaining water and spread out to dry on absorbent paper.

3. Heat the sesame oil in a wok or large frying pan, add the chilli, ginger, mushrooms and Parma ham and stir-fry over a high heat for 2–3 minutes. Add the jam, spring onions and sun-dried tomatoes and bring to the boil. Add the cracked wheat and season to taste with salt, pepper and lemon juice. Heat thoroughly and stir in the pinenuts and cucumber. Keep warm.

4. Heat the oil in a frying pan, add the pigeon breasts in batches and fry for 3 minutes. Turn and cook for 2 further minutes until browned but pink inside.

5. To serve: place 2 pigeon breasts on each of 6 individual plates and spoon a portion of the cracked wheat salad beside each serving. Sprinkle with the chives.

ALSACE GEWÜRZTRAMINER

ASPARAGUS WITH PEANUT SAUCE

(see page 47)

**WARM PIGEON BREAST AND
CRACKED WHEAT SALAD**

**PRUNE AND CHOCOLATE
PUDDINGS**

(see page 167)

Warm Calves' Liver Salad with Kumquats and Walnuts

SERVES 6

900g/2lb calves' liver

1 small head of frisée lettuce

1 bunch of watercress

2 heads of chicory

1 small head of oakleaf lettuce

2 tablespoons walnut oil

1 tablespoon clear honey

1 tablespoon balsamic vinegar

2 tablespoons orange juice

170g/7oz kumquats, thinly sliced

110g/4oz pickled walnuts, roughly chopped

5 spring onions, sliced on the diagonal

1 bunch of chervil, roughly chopped

salt and freshly ground black pepper

3 tablespoons French dressing (see page 190)

1. Trim the calves' liver, removing any membranes and large tubes. Cut into long strips 1cm/½in thick.

2. Tear the salad leaves into bite-sized pieces and mix together.

3. Heat the walnut oil in a large frying pan, add the calves' liver and cook until brown on the outside and pink in the middle. Remove from the pan with a slotted spoon and keep warm.

4. Add the honey, vinegar and orange juice to the pan with the kumquats and cook until the sauce is syrupy and the kumquats softened and beginning to caramelize. Add a little water if the sauce becomes too thick.

5. Add the liver, walnuts and spring onions to the pan and heat through. Season with salt and pepper.

6. Pour the French dressing over the salad leaves and chervil and mix thoroughly.

7. To serve: divide the salad leaves between 6 individual plates. Pile the calves' liver mixture on top and serve immediately.

HUNGARIAN BULL'S BLOOD

CEVICHE

(see page 34)

WARM CALVES' LIVER SALAD
WITH KUMQUATS AND WALNUTS

RUBY RED FRUIT PARCELS

(see page 158)

PASTA

There are literally hundreds of pasta shapes although only about 50 are now produced commercially. We have given a suggestion for each recipe, but do not be afraid to use your own favourite shape. Bear in mind that the Italians are very firm about matching the right pasta and sauce. Pasta like spaghetti and paglia e fieno need oily sauces to coat and lubricate the strands, and do not hold chunky meat or vegetables sauces well. Pasta shells and tubes such as macaroni and penne are perfect with creamy sauces which get caught in the curves and hollows.

There is a tremendous difference between fresh and dried pasta, but dried pasta is by no means the second choice. Fresh pasta, made with flour and eggs, is softer and absorbs sauces more easily. It is lighter in texture and excellent with butter, cream and delicate flavours. Dried pasta is generally made from semolina flour and water, although dried egg pasta is also available. It is a much more robust pasta, with a firmer texture, and should be used with gutsy, stronger flavoured sauces.

Pasta machines are now readily available for making pasta at home, and a hand-cranked machine is relatively inexpensive. These have rollers, rather like a mangle, through which you put the dough, and a dial, which narrows the gap between the rollers as you roll, making the dough thinner.

Pasta must always be cooked in plenty of boiling water to allow it to move around and not stick together. Cooking times vary according to whether it is fresh or dried, and how thick it is. Generally fresh pasta takes much less time to cook and all pasta should be tested by tasting it. It should be *al dente*, or firm between the teeth. It is worth testing dried pasta 5 minutes before the end of the manufacturers' recommended cooking time as they sometimes advise cooking it too long. Remember too that pasta continues cooking as long as it is hot. Drain the pasta in a colander, but not completely. Pasta should always have some of the cooking water clinging to it to keep it moist.

Cracked Black Pepper Pasta with Truffle Oil and Parmesan

SERVES 6

675g/1½lb strong flour

a pinch of salt

2 tablespoons black peppercorns

6 eggs

3 tablespoons oil

4 tablespoons truffle-flavoured oil

3 tablespoons olive oil

170g/6oz Parmesan cheese

1. Make the pasta: put the flour, salt and peppercorns into a food processor and process until the peppercorns are finely chopped. They should not look like ground pepper, but if the pieces are too large they will not go through the pasta machine.

2. Mix the eggs and oil together, and with the motor still running, gradually add them to the flour until the mixture looks like breadcrumbs. Bring a small amount of the mixture together with your fingertips. It should come together easily, but not be too wet. If it does feel wet, add a little more flour.

3. Knead the dough briefly to bring it together, wrap it in clingfilm and leave it to relax for 10 minutes. Then feed it through the widest setting of a pasta machine three or four times before rolling it in the normal way down to the narrowest setting. Cut the pasta to the required shape, either using the machine or by hand. Unroll it and leave to dry, either over a clean broom handle or on a dry tea towel.

4. Bring a large saucepan of salted water, with the remaining oil added, to the boil and drop in the pasta. Give it a stir to prevent it from sticking and boil gently until the pasta is *al dente* (just firm to the bite). This will take anything from 2 to 5 minutes, depending on the thickness of your pasta.

5. Meanwhile, make shavings of Parmesan by running the blade of a swivel-headed vegetable peeler over the surface of the cheese.

6. When the pasta is cooked, drain it thoroughly and transfer to a large serving dish. Pour over the truffle oil and olive oil and toss together, sprinkling the Parmesan over the top. Serve immediately.

BAROLO

PARMA HAM WITH FIG CHUTNEY

(see page 52)

CRACKED BLACK PEPPER PASTA WITH TRUFFLE OIL

PEAR AND MASCARPONE PUFFS

(see page 152)

Three Pea Pasta

SERVES 6

2 tablespoons extra virgin olive oil

1 Spanish onion, sliced

110g/4oz frozen peas

1 teaspoon caster sugar

225g/8oz sugar-snap peas

225g/8oz mangetout

85g/3oz pancetta or rindless streaky bacon, diced

75ml/3fl oz dry white wine

1 head of Little Gem lettuce, washed and shredded

1 large sprig of basil, shredded

250g/9oz mascarpone cheese

675g/1½lb penne

CRAB CAKES WITH HORSERADISH
RELISH
(see page 29)

THREE PEA PASTA

LEMON CURD ICE CREAM
(see page 172)

1. Heat 1 tablespoon of the oil in a frying pan, add the onions and sweat until soft but not brown.

2. Meanwhile, cook the frozen peas in simmering salted water to which the sugar has been added, until tender. Drain the peas, refresh under running cold water, dry thoroughly on absorbent paper and liquidize to a smooth purée.

3. Cook the sugar-snap peas in simmering salted water for 2 minutes. Add the mangetout and cook for 2 further minutes or until tender. Drain, refresh under running cold water and dry thoroughly on absorbent paper.

4. Add the pancetta or bacon to the onions and fry over a low heat, without allowing the onions to colour. Add the wine and reduce by boiling rapidly to about 2 tablespoons.

5. Add the mascarpone and reduce by boiling until syrupy, stirring to prevent the mixture from sticking. Add the pea purée, sugar-snaps and mangetout and heat through thoroughly. Stir in the lettuce and basil and season to taste with salt and pepper.

6. Meanwhile, cook the penne in a large pan of boiling salted water to which the remaining oil has been added, until *al dente*. Drain, return to the pan and toss with the warm pea sauce. Transfer to a large serving dish and serve immediately.

AUSTRALIAN RIESLING

Caramelized Radicchio Pasta

SERVES 6

6 medium heads of radicchio

4 tablespoons extra virgin olive oil

450g/1lb shallots, roughly chopped

3 cloves of garlic, crushed

100ml/3½fl oz dry vermouth

1 tablespoon soft brown sugar

150ml/5fl oz double cream

salt and freshly ground black pepper

675g/1½lb farfalle

TO GARNISH

2 tablespoons freshly grated Parmesan cheese

1. Remove and discard the outer radicchio leaves and cut each head into 8, retaining the core to hold the wedges together.

2. Heat 3 tablespoons of the oil in a large frying pan, add the shallots and sweat until soft. Add the radicchio, garlic and vermouth and reduce by boiling rapidly to 2 tablespoons.

3. Add the sugar to the pan and cook, stirring constantly, until the shallots and radicchio are a rich caramel colour.

4. Add the cream and reduce by boiling rapidly to a coating consistency. Season to taste with salt and pepper.

5. Meanwhile, cook the farfalle in a large saucepan of boiling salted water to which the remaining oil has been added, until *al dente*. Drain, return to the pan and toss with the radicchio sauce. Transfer to a large serving dish, sprinkle over the Parmesan cheese and serve immediately.

BEAUJOLAIS

↩

PROSCIUTTO AND CANNELLINI
BEAN SOUP
(see page 12)

CARAMELIZED RADICCHIO PASTA

CHESTNUT PUDDINGS
(see page 155)

↩

Mushroom and Mascarpone Pasta

SERVES 6

3 tablespoons olive oil

2 onions, finely chopped

450g/1lb field mushrooms

225g/8oz oyster mushrooms, sliced

150ml/5fl oz Madeira

150ml/5fl oz dry white wine

250g/9oz mascarpone cheese

salt and freshly ground black pepper

675kg/1½lb tagliatelle

TO GARNISH

1 bunch of chives, snipped

55g/2oz Parmesan cheese, freshly grated

1. Heat 2 tablespoons of the oil in a large, heavy-bottomed frying pan, add the onion and sweat until soft but not coloured.

2. Add the mushrooms to the pan and cook for 2–3 minutes or until soft. Add the Madeira and white wine and bring to the boil, then reduce the heat and simmer gently until the liquid has reduced by half. Reduce the heat again and add the mascarpone. Continue to simmer until the sauce has reduced again by half. Season to taste with salt and pepper.

3. Meanwhile, cook the tagliatelle in a large saucepan of boiling salted water to which the remaining oil has been added, until *al dente*. Drain, return to the pan and toss with the mushroom sauce. Transfer to a large serving dish, sprinkle over the chives and Parmesan cheese and serve immediately.

POMEROL

SALMON RILLETTES

(see page 28)

MUSHROOM AND
MASCARPONE PASTA

FRIED PEARS WITH
MACADAMIAS AND PINENUTS

(see page 161)

Dried Mushroom and Feta Cheese Pasta

SERVES 6

20g/¾oz dried mushrooms

2 tablespoons oil from feta cheese jar (see below)

1 Spanish onion, finely chopped

3 cloves of garlic, crushed

675g/1½lb pasta shells

1 tablespoon oil

2 × 300g/11oz jars of marinated, cubed feta cheese

3 tablespoons finely chopped marjoram

3 tablespoons double cream

salt and freshly ground black pepper

1. Put the mushrooms into a small bowl and pour over enough boiling water just to cover. Leave to soak for 20 minutes.

2. Meanwhile, heat the feta oil in a saucepan, add the onion and garlic and sweat until soft but not coloured.

3. Drain the mushrooms, reserving the soaking liquid, and chop finely. Strain the liquid through a very fine sieve into the onions, add the mushrooms and reduce by boiling rapidly until syrupy.

4. Meanwhile, cook the pasta shells in a large saucepan of boiling salted water to which 1 tablespoon oil has been added, until *al dente*. Drain and return to the pan. Add the onion and mushroom mixture, feta cheese, marjoram and cream and season to taste with salt and pepper. Transfer to a large serving dish and serve immediately.

MONTEPULCIANO D'ABRUZZO

WARM SEAFOOD SALAD WITH
GREEN CHILLI AND CORIANDER
(see page 30)

DRIED MUSHROOM AND FETA
CHEESE PASTA

LEMON SYLLABUB
(see page 170)

Green Olive and Lemon Pasta

SERVES 6

3 tablespoons good-quality olive oil

1 Spanish onion, finely chopped

½ teaspoon ground cumin

½ teaspoon ground coriander

2 yellow peppers, deseeded and chopped

675g/1½lb farfalle

finely grated zest and juice of 1 lemon

110g/4oz green olives, pitted

1 × 165g/6oz jar of green olive paste

1 tablespoon chopped marjoram

salt and freshly ground black pepper

1. Heat the 2 tablespoons of oil in a frying pan, add the onion and sweat until soft but not coloured. Add the spices and cook for 2–3 further minutes. Add the yellow peppers and cook until soft.

2. Meanwhile, cook the farfalle in a large saucepan of boiling salted water to which the remaining oil has been added, until *al dente*. Drain and return to the pan. Stir in the onion mixture together with the lemon zest, olives, olive paste and marjoram. Season to taste with salt, pepper and lemon juice. Transfer to a large serving dish and serve immediately.

GAVI

SWEET AND SPICY AUBERGINE
KEBABS
(see 44)

GREEN OLIVE AND LEMON PASTA

CHESTNUT PUDDINGS
(see page 155)

Fresh Herb Pasta

SERVES 6

at least 110g/4oz fresh herbs, washed and
destalked, such as sage, thyme, parsley and
rosemary; or dill, chervil, parsley and thyme; or
tarragon, parsley and chervil; or oregano, basil,
thyme, rosemary and parsley
2 cloves of garlic
675g/1½lb paglia e fieno
7 tablespoons extra virgin olive oil
salt and freshly ground black pepper
110g/4oz pinenuts, toasted
110g/4oz Parmesan cheese, freshly grated

1. Put the herbs and garlic into a food processor and process until finely chopped.

2. Meanwhile, cook the paglia e fieno in a large saucepan of boiling salted water to which 1 tablespoon oil has been added, until *al dente*. Drain, return to the pan and add the herbs and remaining oil. Mix thoroughly and season to taste with salt and pepper. Transfer to a large serving dish and serve immediately with the pinenuts and Parmesan cheese handed separately.

PINOT GRIGIO

BLOODY MARY CRAB SALAD

(see page 18)

FRESH HERB PASTA

LEMON AND RASPBERRY
CRÈMES

(see page 156)

Pumpkin and Pecan Pasta

SERVES 6

3 tablespoons good-quality olive oil

1 Spanish onion, finely chopped

900g/2lb pumpkin or squash, peeled, deseeded and
*   chopped*

1 tablespoon finely chopped thyme

3 tablespoons dry sherry

1 tablespoon balsamic or red wine vinegar

4 tablespoons crème fraîche

salt and freshly ground black pepper

675g/1½lb tagliatelle

85g/3oz pecans, roughly chopped

TO GARNISH

shavings of Parmesan cheese

1 tablespoon finely chopped parsley

1. Heat 2 tablespoons of the oil in a large frying pan with a lid, add the onion and sweat until soft but not coloured. Add the pumpkin or squash and thyme, cover and cook for about 10–15 minutes or until the pumpkin or squash is soft but still holding its shape.

2. Add the sherry and vinegar to the pan and reduce by boiling rapidly until syrupy.

3. Add the crème fraîche and reduce again by half. Season to taste with salt and pepper.

4. Meanwhile, cook the tagliatelle in a large saucepan of boiling salted water, until *al dente*. Drain and return to the pan. Add the pumpkin or squash mixture and stir in the pecans. Transfer to a large serving dish, sprinkle with the Parmesan cheese and parsley and serve immediately.

ALSACE PINOT GRIS

GRILLED TIGER PRAWNS
WITH CORIANDER PESTO
(see page 31)

PUMPKIN AND PECAN PASTA

WINTER FRUIT SALAD
(see page 174)

Ravioli with Asparagus

This recipe uses commercially prepared ravioli which is available in most supermarkets and delicatessens.

SERVES 6

900g/2lb asparagus, peeled and trimmed

200g/7oz crème fraîche or Greek yoghurt

salt and freshly ground black pepper

15g/½oz butter

1 onion, thinly sliced

85g/3oz rindless streaky bacon or Parma ham,
   diced (optional)

750–900g/1¾–2lb spinach and ricotta ravioli

1 tablespoon oil

TO GARNISH

shavings of Parmesan cheese

1. Cut the tips off the asparagus and reserve. Cook the asparagus stalks in a large saucepan of boiling salted water until tender. Drain well. Put into a food processor and proceed until smooth, then mix with the crème fraîche or yoghurt. Season to taste with salt and pepper.

2. Melt the butter in a large frying pan, add the onion and bacon or ham, if used, and sweat until soft but not coloured. Mix with the asparagus purée.

3. Cook the asparagus tips in a pan of boiling salted water until tender. Drain and dry carefully on absorbent paper.

4. Meanwhile, cook the ravioli in a large saucepan of boiling salted water to which the oil has been added, until *al dente*. Drain and mix with the asparagus purée and tips. Transfer to a large serving dish, sprinkle with Parmesan cheese and serve immediately.

AUSTRALIAN CHARDONNAY

HOME-MADE GRAVADLAX
WITH PICKLED CUCUMBER

(see page 36)

RAVIOLI WITH ASPARAGUS

PASSIONFRUIT AND MUSCAT
SYLLABUB
(see page 169)

Sun-dried and Cherry Tomato Pasta

SERVES 6

2 tablespoons oil from sun-dried tomatoes (see below)

6 spring onions, sliced

2 cloves of garlic, crushed

2 large sprigs of thyme

200g/7oz sun-dried tomatoes in oil, drained and sliced

900g/2lb cherry tomatoes, halved

675g/1½lb pasta shells

1 tablespoon oil

200g/7oz crème fraîche

salt and freshly ground black pepper

TO GARNISH

shavings of Parmesan cheese

1. Heat the tomato oil in a large saucepan, add the spring onions, garlic and thyme and sweat until the onions are soft.

2. Add the sun-dried and cherry tomatoes and cook for 1 further minute. Season to taste with salt and pepper and remove and discard the thyme.

3. Meanwhile, cook the pasta shells in a large saucepan of boiling salted water to which the oil has been added, until *al dente*. Drain and return to the pan. Add the tomato mixture and the crème fraîche and mix carefully, trying not to break up the cherry tomatoes. Season to taste with salt and pepper. Transfer to a large serving dish, sprinkle with the Parmesan cheese and serve immediately.

CHIANTI CLASSICO

↩

WARM CURRIED CHICKEN LIVER SALAD
(see page 22)

SUN-DRIED AND CHERRY TOMATO PASTA

PEAR AND MASCARPONE PUFFS
(see page 152)

↩

Three-Cheese Pasta

SERVES 6

30g/1oz butter

1 large Spanish onion, finely chopped

170g/6oz Gorgonzola cheese

150ml/5fl oz Greek yoghurt

150ml/5fl oz mascarpone cheese

675g/1½lb paglia e fieno

1 tablespoon oil

55g/2oz unsalted, shelled pistachio nuts

110g/4oz Parmesan cheese, freshly grated

salt and freshly ground black pepper

1. Melt the butter in a large saucepan, add the onion and sweat until soft but not coloured.

2. Cut the Gorgonzola cheese into small cubes, put into a bowl and add the yoghurt and mascarpone. Leave to stand for 20 minutes.

3. Meanwhile, cook the paglia e fieno in a large saucepan of boiling salted water to which the oil has been added, until *al dente*. Drain and return to the pan. Add the onion and cheese mixtures and stir over a low heat until the cheese begins to melt. Add the pistachio nuts and Parmesan cheese and a little water if the mixture is very thick. Season to taste with salt and pepper. Transfer to a large serving dish and serve immediately.

VALPOLICELLA

SPINACH AND BACON SALAD
WITH RED CHILLI AND MANGO

(see page 20)

THREE-CHEESE PASTA

GLAZED FRUITS AND CHESTNUTS
IN MADEIRA SYRUP

(see page 159)

Salmon Pasta with Vermouth and Tarragon

SERVES 6

675g/1½lb salmon fillet, skinned and boned
oil
salt and freshly ground black pepper
5 sprigs of tarragon
100ml/3½fl oz dry white vermouth
675g/1½lb linguine
200ml/7fl oz crème fraîche or mascarpone cheese

TO GARNISH

1 tablespoon snipped chives

1. Preheat the oven to 200°C/400°F/gas mark 6.

2. Trim the salmon fillet and remove any bones.

3. Oil a large sheet of kitchen foil lightly and put the salmon on it. Season with salt and pepper and lay on 3 of the sprigs of tarragon. Pour over the vermouth and make a loose but tightly sealed parcel with the foil. Put on to a baking sheet and bake in the oven for 15 minutes or until cooked.

4. Chop the remaining tarragon finely.

5. Meanwhile, cook the linguine in a large saucepan of boiling salted water to which 1 tablespoon oil has been added, until *al dente*. Drain and keep warm.

6. Remove the salmon from the foil and break into large flakes. Pour the cooking juices into a saucepan and reduce by boiling rapidly to 1 tablespoon. Add to the linguine with the flaked salmon, crème fraîche or mascarpone and the chopped tarragon and season to taste with salt and pepper. Transfer to a large serving dish, sprinkle with the chives and serve immediately.

NEW ZEALAND SAUVIGNON BLANC

ASPARAGUS WITH PEANUT SAUCE
(see page 47)

SALMON PASTA WITH VERMOUTH
AND TARRAGON

SUMMER RED FRUITS
MACERATED IN ELDERFLOWER
CORDIAL AND KIRSCH
(see page 164)

Sorrel, Egg and Anchovy Pasta

SERVES 6

675g/1½lb paglia e fieno
1 tablespoon oil
6 egg yolks
55g/2oz sorrel, chopped
24 anchovy fillets, mashed
3 tablespoons single cream
85g/3oz Parmesan cheese, freshly grated
freshly ground black pepper

1. Cook the pasta in a large saucepan of boiling salted water to which the oil has been added, until *al dente*.

2. Meanwhile, whisk the egg yolks in a bowl and add the sorrel, anchovies, cream and half the Parmesan cheese. Season to taste with pepper.

3. Drain the pasta and return to the pan. Add the egg mixture and put over a medium heat until the eggs are just beginning to cook. Transfer to a large serving dish and serve immediately.

CÔTES DU RHÔNE

CHILLI SQUID SALAD

(see page 35)

SORREL, EGG AND ANCHOVY
PASTA

APPLES WITH CARAMELIZED
CRESCENTS
(see page 160)

Smoked Haddock and Egg Pasta

SERVES 6

150ml/5fl oz double cream

1 slice of onion

2 bay leaves

8 black peppercorns

a pinch of saffron strands

150ml/5fl oz water

450g/1lb smoked haddock

675g/1½lb spaghetti

1 tablespoon oil

6 eggs

85g/3oz Gruyère cheese, grated

freshly ground black pepper

85g/3oz Parmesan cheese, freshly grated

SPICED OLIVE AND CHERRY
TOMATO SALAD
(see page 16)

SMOKED HADDOCK AND
EGG PASTA

MACERATED STRAWBERRIES
(see page 165)

1. Put the cream into a large saucepan with the onion, bay leaves, peppercorns, saffron and water and bring slowly to the boil. Remove from the heat and leave to infuse for 10 minutes.

2. Add the smoked haddock to the pan and poach gently for 10 minutes or until the fish is cooked.

3. Meanwhile, cook the spaghetti in a large saucepan of boiling salted water to which the oil has been added, until *al dente*. Drain thoroughly and return to the pan.

4. Meanwhile, lift the smoked haddock from the cooking liquid and discard the flavouring ingredients. Reduce the liquid by boiling rapidly to half the original quantity. Skin, bone and flake the fish.

5. Beat the eggs, add the Gruyère cheese and season to taste with pepper. Stir the mixture into the spaghetti and cook over a medium heat until the eggs are just beginning to cook. Stir in the smoked haddock and the reduced cream. Transfer to a large serving dish and sprinkle with half the Parmesan cheese. Serve immediately, with the remaining cheese handed separately.

AUSTRALIAN CHARDONNAY

Chicken, Avocado and Pesto Pasta

SERVES 6

675g/1½lb boneless chicken breasts

1 tablespoon good-quality olive oil

1 medium onion, finely chopped

225ml/8fl oz pesto sauce (see page 192)

150ml/5fl oz crème fraîche

*2 avocado pears, peeled, stoned and cut into 1cm/
½in chunks*

675g/1½lb farfalle

1 tablespoon oil

TO SERVE

110g/4oz Parmesan cheese, freshly grated

1. Remove any skin from the chicken and cut into strips.

2. Heat the oil in a large frying pan, add the onion and sweat until soft but not coloured.

3. Add the chicken strips and fry, turning frequently, until cooked through.

4. Stir in the pesto sauce and crème fraîche, then add the avocado and season to taste with salt and pepper.

5. Meanwhile, in a large saucepan of boiling salted water to which the oil has been added, cook the farfalle until *al dente*. Drain and return to the pan. Pour the sauce over and mix carefully. Transfer to a large serving dish and serve immediately, with the Parmesan cheese handed separately.

POUILLY-FUME

MUSHROOM PARCELS

(see page 48)

CHICKEN, AVOCADO AND
PESTO PASTA

NECTARINE, STRAWBERRY AND
ALMOND SPONGE

(see page 150)

Artichoke, Mushroom and Parma Ham Pasta

SERVES 6

2 tablespoons extra virgin olive oil

340g/12oz oyster mushrooms, sliced

1 × 400g/14oz tin of artichoke hearts, drained and
   quartered

110g/4oz Parma ham, sliced

1 × 200g/7oz jar of artichoke paste

salt and freshly ground black pepper

675g/1½lb tagliatelle

TO GARNISH

55g/2oz Parmesan cheese, freshly grated

1. Heat 1 tablespoon of the oil in a large frying pan, add the oyster mushrooms and cook for 1–2 minutes or until soft. Add the artichoke hearts, Parma ham and artichoke paste and heat through thoroughly. Season to taste with salt and pepper.

2. Meanwhile, cook the tagliatelle in a large saucepan of boiling salted water to which the remaining oil has been added, until *al dente*. Drain and return to the pan. Add the artichoke mixture and mix thoroughly. Transfer to a large serving dish, sprinkle with the Parmesan cheese and serve immediately.

AUSTRALIAN CHARDONNAY

ROAST AUBERGINE DIP
(see page 23)

ROAST GARLIC DIP
(see page 24)

OLIVE AND CHILLI DIP
(see page 25)

ARTICHOKE, MUSHROOM AND
PARMA HAM PASTA

MACERATED STRAWBERRIES
(see page 165)

Spaghetti Carbonara

SERVES **6**

675g/1½lb spaghetti

2 tablespoons oil

225g/8oz rindless streaky bacon, cut into small strips

6 egg yolks

3 tablespoons single cream

85g/3oz Parmesan cheese, freshly grated

freshly ground black pepper

1. Cook the spaghetti in a large saucepan of boiling salted water to which 1 tablespoon oil has been added, until *al dente*.

2. Put the remaining oil into a fairly large frying pan, add the strips of bacon and fry them over a medium heat until the bacon fat has melted. Remove the pan from the heat, set aside and keep warm.

3. Meanwhile, whisk the egg yolks in a bowl, whisk in the cream and half the Parmesan cheese, and season generously with pepper.

4. Drain the spaghetti and transfer to the pan with the bacon. Place over a medium heat and pour the egg mixture over. Stir quickly, transfer to a large serving dish and serve immediately, with the remaining Parmesan cheese handed separately.

CHIANTI

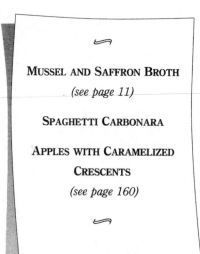

MUSSEL AND SAFFRON BROTH
(see page 11)

SPAGHETTI CARBONARA

APPLES WITH CARAMELIZED CRESCENTS
(see page 160)

Chicken Liver and Lemon Pasta

SERVES 6

675g/1½lb chicken livers
110g/4oz butter
8 spring onions, sliced
1 sprig of thyme
1 clove of garlic, crushed
salt and freshly ground black pepper
2 tablespoons brandy or Marsala
finely grated zest of 2 lemons
675g/1½lb tagliatelle
1 tablespoon oil

TO GARNISH

30g/1oz Parmesan cheese, freshly grated

⤻

SALMON RILLETTES

(see page 28)

**CHICKEN LIVER AND
LEMON PASTA**

**NECTARINE, STRAWBERRY AND
ALMOND SPONGE**

(see page 150)

⤻

1. Trim the chicken livers, removing any greenish parts. Rinse and pat dry with absorbent paper.

2. Melt half the butter in a large frying pan, add the spring onions and thyme and sweat until the onions are soft but not coloured. Add the garlic and cook for 1 further minute.

3. Add half the chicken livers and cook, turning frequently, until brown on the outside but still pink in the centre. Remove and discard the sprig of thyme. Put the chicken liver mixture into a food processor and process until smooth. Season to taste with salt and pepper.

4. Meanwhile, heat the remaining butter in the frying pan until foaming and cook the remaining chicken livers as before. Add the brandy or Marsala and lemon zest to the pan and cook for 1 further minute. Season lightly with salt and pepper and return the processed chicken liver mixture to the pan. Mix thoroughly.

5. Meanwhile, cook the tagliatelle in a large saucepan of boiling salted water to which the oil has been added, until *al dente*. Drain and return to the pan. Add the chicken liver mixture and mix thoroughly. Transfer to a large serving dish, sprinkle with the Parmesan cheese and serve immediately.

RED CÔTES DU LUBÉRON

VEGETABLES

Our quantities have been based on the assumption that guests will have one farinaceous and one 'green' vegetable. Salad could be served afterwards.

The microwave is excellent for many vegetables, ensuring they retain colour, shade and texture. Microwaving is a quick method of cooking and therefore retains more vitamins and minerals.

Quantity for 6	Vegetable	Preparation	Suggested Cooking Method	Approx. Cooking Time	Suggested Garnish/ Sauce
675g/1½lb	**Asparagus**	Wash, remove hard ends and peel tough outer skin if necessary. Tie in bundles.	Steam or boil in unsalted water. Stems will cook slower than heads so stand bundles upright with heads above water level (where they will cook slowly in the steam while the stems cook fast in the boiling water). Char-grill.	6 mins	Walnut oil; Hollandaise sauce or melted butter with pepper, lemon and spring onions; French dressing; mayonnaise; chilli oil; sesame oil and toasted seeds; olive oil and Parmesan shavings.
2 as part of a side dish; 3 as first course	**Avocado**	Peel and remove stone. Slice, cube or halve.			French dressing; tomato, mozzarella, black olives and basil; pesto; Greek yoghurt, Tabasco and finely chopped tomato; soured cream and mock (or real) caviar; lemon juice.
675g/1½lb	**Baby corn**	Wash and trim.	Boil in salted water. Grill. Stir-fry.	5 mins	Melted butter and freshly ground black pepper. Chilli oil; hazelnut oil; balsamic vinegar.
675g/1½lb	**Bean sprouts**	Wash, pick over and drain.	Blanch and refresh. Stir-fry.	10 secs	In salads with French dressing (see page 190)

Quantity for 6	Vegetable	Preparation	Suggested Cooking Method	Approx. Cooking Time	Suggested Garnish/ Sauce
2.3kg/5lb in pods	**Beans, broad**	Shell. (If very young they are good boiled whole.)	Boil in salted water. Remove outer skins after cooking if tough.	7–10 mins	Melted butter and fried bacon pieces or fried chopped walnuts.
675g/1½lb	**Beans, French**	Wash, top and tail. String if necessary.	Boil in salted water.	4 mins	Melted butter and/or fried almonds.
900g/2lb	**Beans, runner**	String if necessary. Wash. Cut into 5cm/2in lengths.	Boil in salted water.	4–7 mins	Melted butter, chopped thyme.
1.1kg/ 2½lb	**Beetroot, young and very small**	Wash but do not peel.	Boil in salted water, then peel.	1 hr	Hot with melted butter; chopped onion, black pepper. Cold with mango.
		Peel, slice or grate.	Fry in butter and lemon.	1–2 mins	Balsamic vinegar.
900g/2lb	**Broccoli**	Wash. Remove tough leaves or stalks.	Boil in salted water.	6–8 mins	Melted butter or olive oil, lemon juice. Parmesan; pinenuts; or balsamic vinegar.
900g/2lb	**Broccoli, sprouting**	Wash. Remove hard stalks.	Boil in salted water.	6–10 mins	Melted butter or blue cheese; slivers of sun-dried tomato or chilli oil.
900g/2lb	**Brussels sprouts**	Trim off tough outer leaves. Trim stalks.	Boil in salted water.	6–12 mins	Melted butter and a pinch of nutmeg or caraway seeds; chestnuts; flaked almond and lemon juice.

Quantity for 6	Vegetable	Preparation	Suggested Cooking Method	Approx. Cooking Time	Suggested Garnish/ Sauce
900g/2lb	**Cabbage, Chinese**	Wash. Slice thickly.	Stir-fry, sweat or boil very briefly. Leave raw.	2 mins	Melted butter, squeeze of lemon, black pepper. Yoghurt and ground cumin.
900g/2lb	**Cabbage, red**	Shred very finely.	Braise. Leave raw.	1 hr	Apple, vinegar, sultanas and sugar.
900g/2lb	**Cabbage, Savoy**	Wash. Slice thinly.	Boil in very little water.	6 mins	Sun-dried tomatoes; Parma ham; pinenuts.
900g/2lb	**Cabbage, spring**	Wash. Shred very finely.	Stir-fry or boil in salted water; deep-fry as mock seaweed.	Stir-fry 5 mins; boil 5 mins	Melted butter; caraway seeds; sugar.
900g/2lb	**Cabbage, white**	Wash. Slice thinly.	Boil in very little water. Leave raw.	6 mins	Greek yoghurt; crème fraîche; caraway seeds.
900g/2lb	**Carrots**	Peel and slice or cut into sticks.	Boil in salted water with a pinch of sugar.	8 mins	Melted butter and chopped mint, orange zest and vinegar.
		Peel and grate coarsely. Do not salt.	Stir-fry in butter or good quantity of olive oil.	2 mins	Salt, pepper and a pinch of sugar; poppy seeds; lemon juice and pumpkin seeds; chervil.
1 large/2 small/1 mini one each	**Cauliflower**	Wash. Break into florets. Remove large stalks.	Boil in salted water.	12 mins	Browned butter (beurre noisette); warm French dressing.
2 large bulbs	**Celeriac**	Wash and peel. Cut into small sticks, slice or grate.	Stir-fry with bacon.	3 mins	Crisp bacon. Mix with mashed potato.
			Boil in salted water, purée and mash.	3–4 mins	Mayonnaise; Hollandaise sauce; butter and lemon juice; French dressing.
		Cut into chunks.	Steam or boil.	10–15 mins	

Quantity for 6	Vegetable	Preparation	Suggested Cooking Method	Approx. Cooking Time	Suggested Garnish/ Sauce
2 heads/ 900g/2lb	Celery	Wash and cut into 5cm/2in pieces.	Boil in salted water. Stir-fry with cumin.	8 mins 2 mins	Lemon juice, chopped dill and melted butter; grated Parmesan; feta or Gruyère.
1.2–1.35kg/ 2½–3lb	Chard	Wash and pick over.	Boil or steam.	4 mins	Butter, lemon juice; Parmesan.
1 each	Chicory/ Endive	Pull off outer leaves. Cut in half lengthwise.	Blanch . . . then braise or grill.	3–4 mins 30 mins 4–5 mins	French dressing; olive oil, lemon juice, walnuts and sun-dried tomatoes; capers; Feta; ham.
1 each	Courgette	Wash and cut into 1 cm/½in chunks.	Boil in salted water or sweat in olive oil or butter.	4–6 mins 5–10 mins	Melted butter, capers and pinenuts; brown sugar, cinnamon; nutmeg.
		Cut lengthwise into 4.	Roast on a griddle or grill.	Until brown	Feta; Parmesan; balsamic or sherry vinegar.
		Grate coarsely including skin. Do not salt.	Stir-fry in butter or olive oil; hazelnut oil with spices (e.g. cumin, cinnamon).	35 secs	Salt, pepper; cinnamon and balsamic vinegar, sultanas, capers.
2 whole	Cucumber	Slice.	Blanch, refresh, dry and toss in olive oil and lemon juice.	30 secs	Mint; dill; poppy seeds; crème fraîche; cumin; yoghurt.
1 small head each/ 1.35kg/3lb	Fennel	Trim, wash and halve lengthwise. Remove woody core.	Blanch, then griddle. Roast.	10 mins 30 mins	Olive oil, lemon juice, sun-dried tomatoes; Parmesan; pinenuts; basil; chopped oregano.

Quantity for 6	Vegetable	Preparation	Suggested Cooking Method	Approx. Cooking Time	Suggested Garnish/ Sauce
900g/2lb	**Kale, curly**	Wash and remove hard stalks.	Put in a covered saucepan with no extra water. Shake over moderate heat. Drain very well.	6–10 mins	Melted butter, a pinch of nutmeg, black pepper and a squeeze of lemon juice.
2 whole	**Kohl rabi**	Peel and slice thinly.	Blanch.	2 mins	Lemon juice; melted butter; olive oil.
900g/2lb	**Leek**	Wash. Remove outer leaves and tough dark green part. Split if large.	Boil or steam in salted water.	6–10 mins	Melted butter and black pepper; crème fraîche; seed or nut oil.
		Julienne or slice.	Shallow-fry.	4–5 mins	
450g/1lb	**Mangetout**	Wash, top and tail.	Stir-fry or boil.	4–5 mins	Melted butter; olive oil; chopped chilli.
1.35kg/3lb	**Marrow**	Wash and peel if tough-skinned. Cut into 5cm/2in chunks.	Steam.	10 mins	Browned butter (beurre noisette) and chopped parsley, chervil or tarragon.
675g/1½lb	**Mushroom, button/ chestnut/ field**	Do not peel unless very old and tough. Wipe and trim off any ragged stalks. Quarter if large or slice.	Sweat in olive oil or butter with a squeeze of lemon. Grill, brushed with olive oil and garlic.	4–8 mins	Melted butter, black pepper and lemon juice; a little double or soured cream; Boursin or mascarpone; chopped oregano, sage or thyme.
675–900g/ 1½–2lb	**Okra, small and tender**	Wash carefully. Trim off stalks and soak in acidulated water for 1 hour.	Sweat gently with onion and garlic in oil or butter.		Sliced tomato; garlic; lemon juice; melted butter; chopped basil; balsamic or wine vinegar.

Quantity for 6	Vegetable	Preparation	Suggested Cooking Method	Approx. Cooking Time	Suggested Garnish/ Sauce
1 each or 900g/2lb	**Onion, small red/ yellow/ white**	Peel, cut off top and leave whole.	Boil or steam.	15–30 mins	Toss in butter or olive oil and pinch of sugar until pale brown, with sun-dried tomatoes, chopped rosemary and thyme.
		Trim.	Bake and peel after cooking.	30 mins	Melted butter, balsamic vinegar, black pepper.
1.35kg/3lb	**Pak choi**	Wash and pick over. Slice if desired.	Stir-fry or steam.	5 mins	Caraway; sesame or walnut oil; yoghurt; Chinese five-spice powder.
900g/2lb	**Parsnip**	Peel and cut up if large.	Boil in salted water or boil and mash.	20–30 mins	Melted butter, olive oil and black pepper.
			Roast with butter or oil.	40 mins– 1 hr	Parmesan.
1.2kg/ 2½lb	**Pea**	Hull.	Boil in salted water with a good pinch of sugar and a sprig of mint.	5–20 mins	Melted butter; chopped mint; spring onions; Parma ham; lettuce; cherry tomatoes.
3 whole	**Pepper**	Wash, quarter and deseed.	Grill until black. Place in an airtight bag and leave to cool. Peel.		French dressing, chopped basil and oregano; black olives; capers; Parmesan or feta.

Potatoes see page 143

1.35kg/3lb	**Pumpkin and squash**	Wash and peel. Cut into 5cm/2in chunks.	Char-grill with oil.		
			Steam or sweat in butter with oregano or rosemary.	20 mins	Melted butter and chopped parsley; olive oil; French dressing; pinenuts; sesame seeds;
			Roast with butter and lemon juice.	20 mins	sunflower seeds.

Quantity for 6	Vegetable	Preparation	Suggested Cooking Method	Approx. Cooking Time	Suggested Garnish/ Sauce
900g/2lb	**Salsify** (white-skinned)	Wash and cut into 5cm/2in lengths.	Boil. Peel after cooking.	10–15 mins	Browned butter (beurre noisette); grated lemon zest; garlic; chopped thyme, rosemary, tarragon or chervil.
900g/2lb	**Samphire**		Boil in unsalted water, then fry in oil.	4–6 mins	Melted butter and lemon juice; sesame seeds; sun-dried tomato; Parmesan.
16 roots 900g/2lb	**Scorzonera (black-stemmed)**	Wash, peel and cut into 5cm/2in lengths.	Boil, steam or sweat.	10–15 mins	Browned butter (beurre noisette); olive oil; double cream; mushrooms; crème fraîche; lemon juice.
900g/2lb	**Sea kale**	Wash and remove any tough stems.	Boil in salted water or steam.	10–20 mins	Hollandaise sauce or melted butter (seasoned with salt, pepper and lemon juice).
675g/1½lb	**Shallot**	Blanch and peel. Leave whole.	Boil in salted water.	15–20 mins	Browned butter (beurre noisette).
			Steam or sweat.	20 mins	Parmesan; olive oil; red chilli; chopped rosemary or thyme; black pepper.
			Roast (with olive oil/ chilli).	35 mins	
225g/8oz	**Sorrel**	Wash well, pick over and remove older leaves.	Put into a covered pan with a few tablespoons of water. Shake over a moderate heat. Drain and squeeze dry. Chop well.	4 mins	Chopped in dressings or butter sauces; mixed with spinach or tomatoes or lemon juice and Parmesan. With boiled new potatoes and lemon zest in potato salad.
			Raw in salads.		

Quantity for 6	Vegetable	Preparation	Suggested Cooking Method	Approx. Cooking Time	Suggested Garnish/ Sauce
Cooked: 2kg/4½lb	**Spinach**	Wash well. Pull away stalks.	Put into covered saucepan *without any water*. Shake over moderate heat. Drain and squeeze dry.	4 mins	Melted butter and grated nutmeg or crushed fried garlic; lemon juice; sun-dried tomatoes.
Raw. 340g/12oz			Use young leaves raw for salads.		French dressing.
24	**Spring onion**	Wash and peel.	Stir-fry in oil. Use raw in salads.	30 secs	Cherry tomatoes, chopped coriander, sesame oil and seeds.
2 whole/ 900g/2lb	**Swede**	Peel thickly and slice.	Sweat or steam. Mash if very wet and shake over heat to dry.	20–30 mins	Mashed: plenty of butter, salt and pepper. Whole: Melted butter and/or chopped parsley.
1.35kg/3lb	**Sweet potato**	Wash and leave skin on or cut into chunks.	Bake. Roast in chunks with salt.	1 hr	Soured cream, black pepper.
675g/1½lb	**Tomato**	Wash and split in half.	Raw. Grill. Bake, sprinkled with butter, chopped onion and/or garlic.	3 mins 10 mins in moderate oven	Olive oil; Parmesan; chopped basil, parsley; black pepper; salt. Goat's cheese; mozzarella; feta; chopped thyme or oregano, basil.
900g/2lb	**Turnip, small**	Peel thickly if necessary and slice thickly.	Sweat or steam. Mash if very wet and shake over heat to dry.	15 mins	Melted butter, good olive oil and lemon/ orange juice; vinegars.
2–3 bunches	**Watercress**	Wash and pick over.	Raw in salads. Steam.		Sliced oranges. Olive oil or lemon juice.

Quantity per person	Vegetable	Preparation	Suggested Cooking Method	Approx. Cooking Time	Suggested Garnish/ Sauce
2 small or 1 large	**Potato**	Wash and scrub.	Bake: rub with salt and prick all over.	1 hr	Butter, grated cheese; soured cream; cream cheese; yoghurt. Parmesan; grated horseradish; orange zest; mustard powder; chopped coriander, rosemary or thyme.
3 small		Wash, peel and cut into chunks	Roast: blanch 5 mins then scratch all over with fork. If time is short, cut into small 1cm/½in chunks, baste with oil.	1–1½ hrs 50 mins	
170g/6oz 110g/4oz		If new leave whole. Do not peel.	Boil or steam.	12 mins	Melted butter and chopped watercress, chives, mint or thyme; yoghurt; crème fraîche.
170g/6oz		Wash, peel and slice.	Sauté: blanch 5 mins. Fry/sauté slowly in butter.	30 mins	Chopped rosemary or thyme.
110–170g/ 4–6oz			Mash: boil until tender. Drain well. Mash. Beat in warm milk and melted butter.	15–20 mins	Grated nutmeg, salt and black pepper; olive oil in place of milk and butter.

Quantity Staples for 6	Suggested Accompaniments for All Staples
225g/8oz **Couscous**	Beansprouts and alfalfa. Lemon grass, lime leaves.
	Chopped herbs: Mint; dill; thyme; parsley; chives; basil; chervil.
	Vegetables: Asparagus; truffle; spring onion; shallot; mushrooms; new potatoes; fresh chilli; cherry tomatoes; ginger. Green and black olives.
	Oils: Extra virgin olive; chilli; garlic; truffle; sesame oil and toasted seeds; walnut oil and nuts; hazelnut oil and nuts and spring onion; rosemary; basil.
225g/8oz **Cracked wheat/ bulgar/ burghul**	**Vinegars:** Honey; raspberry; sherry; balsamic; rice wine.
	Cheeses: Parmesan; Gruyère; Boursin; feta; goat's.
	Seeds: Pinenuts; sunflower seeds; cashew nuts; peanuts; pecans; pistachio nuts; flaked almonds; chestnuts; pumpkin seeds; poppy seeds.
	Spices: Cinnamon powder and sticks; cumin; chilli and cayenne; paprika; mustard seeds; nutmeg; coriander; caraway; juniper; cardamom; turmeric; saffron; green peppercorns; Tabasco sauce.
250g/9oz **Noodles: wheat; egg; rice; glass/ cellophane**	**Juices:** Lime, lemon, orange and grapefruit with grated zest.
	Creams: Crème fraîche; soured cream.
	Dressings: French dressing; honey; Hollandaise.
	Jars: Capers; anchovies; olives; truffles; lumpfish roe; sun-dried tomatoes; artichokes; water chestnuts.
	Dried: Sultanas; apricots; prunes; cherries; cranberries.
30g/1oz **Puy lentils** per person	
Rice: basmati; long-grain; brown; fragrant; boil-in-the-bag; lemon grass; wild	
55g/2oz per person. For rice salad equal quantity of cold cooked rice to almost any vegetable. Use dressing to moisten, not soak.	

PUDDINGS

INSTANT PUDDINGS

Cream, Yoghurt and Cheese

- Fromage blanc or cream cheese with vanilla sugar served with strawberries, raspberries, blueberries, peaches, nectarines, mangoes or figs.
- Equal quantities fromage frais and sieved cottage cheese sweetened with icing sugar and served with fresh fruit.
- Fromage frais sprinkled with dark brown sugar and served with fresh dates and figs.
- Plain yoghurt and blackcurrant cordial served with strawberries and raspberries.
- Plain yoghurt and passionfruit cordial served with shortbread.
- Equal quantities mascarpone cheese and sweetened chestnut purée swirled together and decorated with sifted cocoa powder.
- Green seedless grapes, halved and sprinkled with elderflower cordial and topped with Greek yoghurt.

Ice Creams and Sorbets

- Always use the very best quality ice cream and serve with shortbread, *langues du chat*, florentines or tuile biscuits.
- Vanilla ice cream with easy chocolate sauce (see page 199), fruit preserves sauce (see page 198), maple syrup or sliced preserved stem ginger and syrup.
- Cinnamon ice cream with caramelized brown breadcrumbs or butterscotch sauce (see page 199).
- Lemon sorbet with crème de cassis or raspberry coulis.
- Blackcurrant sorbet with mango coulis (see page 199).
- Pear sorbet with raspberry coulis or easy chocolate sauce (see page 199).

Fruit

- Mango slices sprinkled with fresh lime juice.
- Fresh figs, quartered, sprinkled with orange juice and chopped mint.
- Fresh figs, quartered, sprinkled with sugar and grilled for 5 minutes.
- Strawberries, halved, sprinkled with rosewater and macerated for 15 minutes.
- Watermelon, peeled, cut into chunks and sprinkled with orangeflower water.
- Banana mashed with double cream, preserved stem ginger and syrup.
- Pears, peeled, cored and thinly sliced and sprinkled with sugar, grated lemon zest and Cointreau. Served with grated chocolate, lychees or roasted hazelnuts.
- Galia, honeydew and watermelon salad with chopped mint.

All-one-colour fruit salads

Red: strawberries, plums, watermelon, raspberries, blueberries, redcurrants, pink grapes.

Green: apples, green grapes, pears, kiwi fruit, greengages, honeydew melon.

Orange: apricots, peaches, Galia melon, orange segments, passionfruit.

Flavourings for fruit salads

Elderflower, blackcurrant or ginger cordial, orangeflower water, rosewater, Kirsch, Poire William, Calvados, Grand Marnier or Cointreau.

HOT PUDDINGS
Mango, Raspberry and Blueberry Clafoutis

SERVES 6

55g/2oz plain flour

a pinch of salt

55g/2oz light muscovado sugar

3 eggs

290ml/½ pint milk

1 tablespoon oil

2 tablespoons Cointreau

finely grated zest of 1 orange

butter for greasing

1 mango, peeled and cut into cubes

225g/8oz raspberries

150g/5oz blueberries

> SMOKED HALIBUT PÂTÉ
> *(see page 27)*
>
> CHICKEN SAUTÉ WITH
> ARTICHOKES AND SUN-DRIED
> TOMATOES
> *(see page 75)*
>
> MANGO, RASPBERRY AND
> BLUEBERRY CLAFOUTIS

TO FINISH

icing sugar

1. Preheat the oven to 180°C/350°F/gas mark 4.

2. Sift the flour and salt into a large bowl and add the sugar. Make a well in the centre and break the eggs into it.

3. Beat the eggs with a wooden spoon, gradually drawing in the flour. Beat in the milk gradually until the batter is smooth. Add the oil, Cointreau and orange zest and refrigerate for 30 minutes.

4. Butter a shallow ovenproof dish and put all the fruits into the bottom. Pour in the batter, covering the fruits.

5. Bake in the oven for 40 minutes, then lower the temperature to 150°C/300°F/gas mark 2 and bake for 30–40 further minutes. The clafoutis is cooked when a skewer or sharp knife inserted into the centre comes out clean.

6. Serve warm, lightly dusted with icing sugar.

COTEAUX DE LAYON

Nectarine, Strawberry and Almond Sponge

To prevent the sponge mixture from curdling and to give a light result, use eggs at room temperature.

SERVES 6

2 nectarines, stoned

340g/12oz strawberries, hulled

butter for greasing

finely grated zest of 1 orange

1 teaspoon finely chopped rosemary

140g/5oz light muscovado sugar

110g/4oz butter, softened

2 eggs, beaten

55g/2oz ground almonds

110g/4oz self-raising flour

a pinch of salt

2 tablespoons Amaretto or Kirsch (optional)

30g/1oz flaked almonds

1. Preheat the oven to 200°C/400°F/gas mark 6.
2. Chop the fruit into 1cm/½in pieces. Lightly butter a pie dish, add the fruit and sprinkle with half the orange zest, the rosemary and 30g/1oz of the sugar.
3. Cream the butter until soft and beat in the remaining sugar until light and fluffy. Add the eggs gradually and sift in the almonds, flour and salt. Mix until smooth with the remaining orange zest, the Amaretto or Kirsch, if used, and enough water to achieve a dropping consistency. Spread the mixture over the fruit and scatter over the almonds.
4. Bake in the oven for 25 minutes or until the sponge is firm to the touch and golden-brown. Serve warm.

SAUTERNES

SPRING VEGETABLES IN
THAI-STYLE DRESSING
(see page 45)

SALMON FILLET WITH
VODKA AND LIME
(see page 59)

NECTARINE, STRAWBERRY
AND ALMOND SPONGE

Baked Bananas in Amaretti Crumble

SERVES 6

15g/½oz butter

9 firm bananas

3 cardamom pods, seeds removed and crushed

½ teaspoon ground cinnamon

2 tablespoons dark muscovado sugar

finely grated zest and juice of 1 orange

2 tablespoons Amaretto or Kirsch (optional)

FOR THE CRUMBLE

85g/3oz plain flour

a pinch of salt

55g/2oz butter

30g/1oz caster sugar

110g/4oz Amaretti biscuits, crushed

1. Preheat the oven to 190°C/375°F/gas mark 5.

2. Grease a shallow ovenproof dish with the butter.

3. Peel and halve the bananas lengthwise. Put into an ovenproof dish with the cardamon seeds, cinnamon, sugar, orange zest and juice, and Amaretto or Kirsch, if used.

4. Sift the flour and salt into a bowl and rub in the butter until the mixture resembles coarse breadcrumbs. Mix in the sugar and crushed biscuits. Sprinkle the mixture over the bananas.

5. Put on to a baking sheet and bake on the top shelf of the oven for 10 minutes, then lower the temperature to 170°C/325°F/gas mark 3 and bake for 20 further minutes or until the bananas are soft when tested with a skewer. Serve warm.

MADEIRA

╭──────────────────────────────╮

COUSCOUS SALAD WITH GRILLED AUBERGINES

(see page 14)

PORK MEDALLIONS WITH YELLOW PEPPER RELISH

(see page 100)

BAKED BANANAS IN AMARETTI CRUMBLE

╰──────────────────────────────╯

Pear and Mascarpone Puffs

These puffs are also delicious with apples and Calvados in place of the pears and Poire William.

SERVES 6

55g/2oz sultanas
2 tablespoons Poire William liqueur
2 ripe pears, Comice or William
450g/1lb puff pastry
150ml/5fl oz mascarpone cheese
2 tablespoons muscovado sugar
a pinch of ground cinnamon
1 egg, beaten with ½ teaspoon sugar

1. Soak the sultanas in the liqueur.

2. Peel, core and chop the pears.

3. Roll out the pastry to the thickness of a 50-pence coin and cut out 6 equal squares. Put a generous spoonful of mascarpone into the centre of each square and scatter over the sultanas, sugar, cinnamon and fruit.

4. Dampen the corners of the pastry with water and bring them up to the centre, pinching the edges tightly to seal.

5. Put on to a baking sheet and brush with the egg glaze. Chill for at least 20 minutes.

6. Preheat the oven to 200°C/400°F/gas mark 6.

7. Bake in the oven for 15–20 minutes. Serve immediately.

VOUVRAY DEMI-SEC

SMOKED HALIBUT WITH
JAPANESE-STYLE CUCUMBER
SALAD
(see page 39)

BEEF STROGANOFF WITH GINGER
AND CHINESE FIVE-SPICE
(see page 89)

PEAR AND MASCARPONE PUFFS

Chocolate Bread and Butter Pudding

SERVES 6

30g/1oz butter, softened

4 slices of chocolate bread or panetone

55g/2oz sultanas

2 eggs

1 egg yolk

150ml/5fl oz full-cream milk

200ml/7fl oz crème fraîche

30g/1oz caster sugar

1 tablespoon brandy

1. Grease a shallow ovenproof dish with a little of the butter, and spread the rest on the slices of bread. Cut the bread in half on the diagonal and put the slices in the bottom of the dish. Sprinkle the sultanas over the bread.

2. Mix together all the remaining ingredients and pour over the bread. Leave to soak for at least 30 minutes.

3. Preheat the oven to 170°C/325°F/gas mark 3. Put the dish into a roasting tin and pour in enough boiling water to come halfway up the sides of the dish. Cook in the oven for 30 minutes or until the custard has just set.

NOTE: Chocolate bread is available in most supermarkets.

MUSCAT DE BEAUMES DE VENISE

MUSSEL AND SAFFRON BROTH
(see page 11)

GLAZED DUCK BREASTS WITH
APPLE AND SAGE CHUTNEY
(see page 80)

CHOCOLATE BREAD AND
BUTTER PUDDING

Chocolate Rum and Raisin Puddings

SERVES 6

55g/2oz raisins

2 tablespoons dark rum

110g/4oz good-quality dark chocolate

4 eggs, separated

55g/2oz plus 1 tablespoon caster sugar

1. Soak the raisins in the rum.

 2. Break the chocolate into even pieces and melt in a heatproof bowl placed over a saucepan of simmering water. Remove from the heat and allow to cool slightly.

3. Meanwhile, put the egg yolks and 55g/ 2oz of the sugar into a bowl and whisk until thick and fluffy. Drain the raisins, reserving the rum, and stir the raisins into the melted chocolate. Add the rum to the egg yolk and sugar mixture and whisk for 5 minutes.

4. Whisk the egg whites to stiff peaks, add the remaining tablespoon of sugar and whisk again until stiff and shiny. Fold the chocolate and raisins into the egg yolk mixture. Stir in a spoonful of the egg whites, to loosen, then fold in the remaining whites. Divide the mixture between 6 ramekins and chill or freeze until ready to cook.

5. Preheat the oven to 200°C/400°F/gas mark 6. Put a baking sheet into the oven to preheat.

6. Put the ramekins on to the hot baking sheet and cook for 15 minutes if chilled or 20 minutes if frozen. Serve immediately.

AUSTRALIAN ORANGE MUSCAT 🍷

MUSHROOMS WITH ARTICHOKE HEARTS AND OLIVES

(see page 50)

PORK NOISETTES WITH PUMPKIN AND CHERRY TOMATO CHUTNEY

(see page 101)

CHOCOLATE RUM AND RAISIN PUDDINGS

Chestnut Puddings

SERVES 6

4 eggs, separated

55g/2oz plus 1 tablespoon caster sugar

2 tablespoons Marsala

1 × 250g/8½oz tin of sweetened chestnut purée

4 marrons glacés, chopped (optional)

1. Whisk the egg yolks and 55g/2oz sugar until very light and fluffy. This may take up to 5 minutes. Add the Marsala and whisk for 5 further minutes.

2. Whisk the egg whites to stiff peaks, add the tablespoon of caster sugar and continue to whisk until very stiff and shiny.

3. Mix the chestnut purée into the egg yolk mixture and stir in the marrons glacés, if used. Stir in a tablespoonful of the egg whites to loosen the mixture, then gently fold in the remaining egg whites. Divide the mixture between 6 ramekins and chill or freeze until ready to cook.

4. Preheat the oven to 200°C/400°F/gas mark 6. Put a baking sheet in the oven to preheat.

5. Put the ramekins on to the hot baking sheet and cook for 15 minutes if chilled or 20 minutes if frozen. Serve immediately.

ASTI SPUMANTE

MUSHROOM PARCELS
(see page 48)

GRILLED CHICKEN WITH
MUSTARD AND CRANBERRIES
(see page 72)

CHESTNUT PUDDINGS

Lemon and Raspberry Crèmes

SERVES 6

4 eggs

1 egg yolk

140g/5oz caster sugar

200g/7oz Greek yoghurt

finely grated zest and juice of 2 lemons

225g/8oz fresh raspberries

6 cardamom pods, seeds removed and crushed

TO FINISH

icing sugar

1. Preheat the oven to 180°C/350°F/gas mark 4.

2. Mix the whole eggs and yolk together briefly and stir in the sugar, yoghurt and lemon juice. Stir together carefully, taking care not to create air bubbles. Strain and stir in the lemon zest.

3. Divide the raspberries between 6 ramekins, sprinkle over the cardamom seeds and pour the lemon mixture over the top.

4. Stand the ramekins in a roasting tin and pour in enough boiling water to come halfway up the sides. Cook in the middle of the oven for 20–25 minutes or until set. Serve warm, dusted with icing sugar.

GERMAN RIESLING BEERENAUSLESE

CUCUMBER AND MELON
GAZPACHO

(see page 7)

SALMON OLIVES WITH
HERB SAUCE

(see page 58)

LEMON AND RASPBERRY
CRÈMES

Honey and Fig Custards

SERVES 6

110g/4oz semi-dried figs or apricots, finely chopped

4 tablespoons Marsala

4 eggs, beaten

40g/1½oz light brown sugar

¼ teaspoon ground cinnamon

55g/2oz clear honey

225g/8oz Greek yoghurt

TO FINISH

ground cinnamon

icing sugar

1. Macerate the figs or apricots in the Marsala overnight.

2. Preheat the oven to 180°C/350°F/gas mark 4.

3. Beat the eggs lightly, add the sugar and cinnamon, stir in the honey and mix in the yoghurt.

4. Divide the figs or apricots between 6 ramekins and strain over the honey mixture.

5. Stand the ramekins in a roasting tin and pour in enough boiling water to come halfway up the sides. Cook in the centre of the oven for 30–35 minutes or until set.

6. Serve warm, dusted with cinnamon and icing sugar.

MADEIRA

INDIVIDUAL RED ONION AND
ROSEMARY SOUFFLÉS
(see page 40)

VENISON STEAKS WITH
CRANBERRIES AND CHESTNUTS
(see page 82)

HONEY AND FIG CUSTARDS

Ruby Red Fruit Parcels

SERVES 6

2 nectarines, stoned

225g/8oz strawberries, hulled

225g/8oz raspberries

110g/4oz blueberries or seedless pink grapes

30g/1oz caster sugar

3 tablespoons ruby port

6 small sprigs of rosemary

TO SERVE

200ml/7fl oz crème fraîche

1. Preheat the oven to 240°C/475°F/gas mark 8.
2. Cut the nectarines into chunks and mix with the remaining fruit.
3. Divide the fruit between 6 × 20cm/8in squares of kitchen foil, sprinkle over the sugar and port and put 1 sprig of rosemary on each.
4. Fold up the edges of the foil to form parcels and put on to a baking sheet. Bake in the oven for 7 minutes.
5. Serve immediately with the crème fraîche.

TAWNY PORT

SMOKED SALMON ON POTATO
AND BUTTERMILK PANCAKES

(see page 38)

CALVES' LIVER WITH GINGER
AND PECAN SAUCE AND
PARSNIP CRISPS

(see page 84)

RUBY RED FRUIT PARCELS

Glazed Fruits and Chestnuts in Madeira Syrup

SERVES 6

225g/8oz tinned or vacuum-packed whole chestnuts

5 tablespoons water

285g/10oz granulated sugar

200ml/7fl oz Madeira

6 dried figs

6 dried pears

6 no-need-to-soak prunes

juice of ½ lemon

TO SERVE

570ml/1 pint rich vanilla ice cream

1. If the chestnuts are tinned, drain and dry on absorbent paper. If they are vacuum-packed, rinse under running cold water to separate, then dry on absorbent paper.

2. Put the water, sugar and Madeira into a heavy-bottomed saucepan. Dissolve the sugar slowly without boiling.

3. When the sugar has dissolved, turn up the heat, bring to the boil and reduce by boiling rapidly until syrupy. Add the chestnuts and dried fruit and simmer for 5–10 minutes or until the syrup is thick, stirring occasionally. Remove from the heat, add the lemon juice and allow to cool slightly.

4. Serve with the ice cream.

MADEIRA

TWICE-BAKED INDIVIDUAL GOAT'S
CHEESE SOUFFLÉS WITH
WALNUT AND PARSLEY SAUCE

(see page 41)

THAI DUCK SALAD

(see page 108)

GLAZED FRUITS AND CHESTNUTS
IN MADEIRA SYRUP

Apples with Caramelized Crescents

SERVES 6

6 dessert apples

170g/5oz caster sugar

450ml/¾ pint water

3 slices of white bread, crusts removed

30g/1oz unsalted butter

1 tablespoon demerara sugar

¼ teaspoon ground cinnamon

finely grated zest of 1 orange (optional)

1 tablespoon Calvados

1. Peel, core and cut each apple into 8.

2. Meanwhile, put the caster sugar and water into a heavy-bottomed saucepan. Dissolve the sugar slowly without boiling. When the sugar has dissolved, turn up the heat and boil rapidly for 3–4 minutes or until syrupy. Put the apples into the syrup and simmer gently for 5 minutes or until glossy and tender.

3. Using a biscuit cutter, cut the bread into large crescent shapes.

4. Put the butter into a large frying pan with the demerara sugar and cinnamon and heat until the sugar has melted. Add the bread crescents and fry over a low heat until golden-brown and caramelized on both sides, taking care that the bread does not burn. Remove from the pan and keep warm.

5. Lift the apple slices from the syrup with a slotted spoon. Add the orange zest, if used, and Calvados to the syrup and continue to reduce by boiling rapidly until thickened.

6. Return the apple slices to the syrup, reheat through and serve with the crescents.

MOSCATEL

THREE-CHEESE PÂTÉ WITH
PECANS

(see page 26)

SALMON STEAKS WITH OYSTER
MUSHROOM AND WHISKY SAUCE

(see page 61)

APPLES WITH CARAMELIZED
CRESCENTS

Fried Pears with Macadamias and Pinenuts

SERVES 6

6 ripe dessert pears, peeled, cored and quartered

2 tablespoons demerara sugar

55g/2oz unsalted butter

85g/3oz macadamia nuts

30g/1oz pinenuts

1 tablespoon very finely chopped rosemary

3 tablespoons clear honey

1 tablespoon lemon juice

TO SERVE

290ml/½ pint Greek yoghurt

4 tablespoons clear honey

1. Sprinkle the pears with the sugar. Heat the butter in a large frying pan, add the pears and cook over a low heat until golden-brown and just soft. Lift on to a serving plate and keep warm.

2. Put the macadamia nuts, pinenuts and rosemary into the frying pan and fry until golden-brown, stirring constantly. Scatter over the pears. Tip off any remaining butter and add the honey and lemon juice to the pan. Bring to the boil and pour over the pears.

3. Mix together the Greek yoghurt and honey and serve immediately with the pears.

HUNGARIAN TOKAY ASZÚ

CARROT AND CUMIN SOUP

(see page 6)

COLLOPS OF LAMB
WITH FLAGEOLET BEANS
AND OYSTER MUSHROOMS

(see page 97)

FRIED PEARS WITH
MACADAMIAS AND PINENUTS

Figs with Goat's Cheese and Pecan Caramel

SERVES 6

12 figs

2 × 150g soft mild goat's cheeses or fromage frais

285g/10oz granulated sugar

150ml/5fl oz water

85g/3oz pecans, chopped

¼ teaspoon freshly ground black pepper

1. Cut the figs almost into quarters to the root end and gently push upwards with finger and thumb to open up.

2. Divide the cheese between the figs, pushing it down into the fruit. Put 2 figs on each of 6 individual plates and refrigerate.

3. Put the sugar and half the water into a heavy-bottomed saucepan and dissolve the sugar slowly without boiling. When the sugar has dissolved, turn up the heat and boil until it is a good caramel colour. Remove from the heat and pour in the remaining water, taking care as the mixture may spit. Add the pecan nuts and pepper.

4. Pour the hot caramel over the figs and serve immediately.

NOTE: The caramel can be made in advance but do not add the nuts. When ready to serve, reheat the caramel with 1 tablespoon water. Bring to the boil and add the pecan nuts and pepper.

TAWNY PORT

~

ASPARAGUS WITH PEANUT SAUCE

(see page 47)

**TOURNEDOS WITH
WILD MUSHROOMS
AND TRUFFLE MASH**

(see page 91)

**FIGS WITH GOAT'S CHEESE
AND PECAN CARAMEL**

~

COLD PUDDINGS

Citrus Fruit Compote with Spiced Caramel

SERVES 6

3 large oranges
1 pink grapefruit
6 kumquats
1 small pineapple

FOR THE SPICED CARAMEL

225g/8oz granulated sugar
290ml/½ pint water
2 bay leaves
2 star anise
1 cinnamon stick
1 tablespoon coriander seeds, crushed
1 strip of lemon zest
*2.5cm/1in piece of fresh root ginger, peeled and
    roughly chopped*

1. Make the spiced caramel: put the sugar and half the water into a heavy-bottomed saucepan and dissolve the sugar slowly without boiling. When the sugar has dissolved, turn up the heat and boil until the melted sugar is a dark caramel colour.

2. Remove from the heat immediately and pour in the remaining water, taking care as the mixture can spit. Add the remaining caramel ingredients to the pan and leave to cool, preferably overnight.

3. Prepare the fruit: peel, removing all pith, and segment the oranges and grapefruit. Slice the kumquats very thinly.

4. Peel and core the pineapple and cut into chunks. Put the fruit into a serving bowl, then strain over the caramel. Chill well before serving.

MADEIRA

ALMOND AND PARSLEY SOUP

(see page 5)

LAMBS' KIDNEYS WITH
RED ONION AND SAGE

(see page 86)

CITRUS FRUIT COMPOTE WITH
SPICED CARAMEL

Summer Red Fruits Macerated in Elderflower Cordial and Kirsch

SERVES 6

1 punnet of strawberries, hulled and halved

2 punnets of raspberries

1 punnet of redcurrants

1 punnet of blueberries

5 tablespoons elderflower cordial

2 tablespoons Kirsch

3 sprigs of young mint leaves

1. Mix all the fruits together carefully and transfer to a large serving dish.

2. Sprinkle over the elderflower cordial and Kirsch and chop the mint leaves, reserving the smallest for decoration. Leave to macerate in the refrigerator for 30 minutes.

3. Decorate with the remaining mint.

COTEAUX DE LAYON

SPICED OLIVE AND CHERRY
TOMATO SALAD

(see page 16)

SALMON FILLET WITH
VODKA AND LIME

(see page 59)

SUMMER RED FRUITS
MACERATED IN ELDERFLOWER
CORDIAL AND KIRSCH

Macerated Strawberries

SERVES 6

670g/1½lb strawberries, hulled

2 tablespoons caster sugar

2 tablespoons Cointreau, Grand Marnier or
*   orangeflower water*

finely grated zest of 1 orange

290ml/½ pint double cream

290ml/½ pint Greek yoghurt

1 tablespoon icing sugar

TO DECORATE

225g/8oz raspberries and/or blueberries

1. Mash the strawberries roughly with a fork on a large plate, mix in the sugar and sprinkle with the liqueur or orangeflower water and the orange zest. Mix thoroughly and pile into a glass serving dish. Leave to macerate for at least 15 minutes.

2. Whip the cream lightly and fold in the yoghurt and icing sugar.

3. Spread carefully over the strawberry mixture. Sprinkle with the raspberries and/or blueberries. Serve immediately.

ROSÉ CHAMPAGNE

WARM PUY LENTIL SALAD
(see page 15)

MONKFISH ON ROSEMARY
SKEWERS
(see page 70)

MACERATED STRAWBERRIES

Marron Glacé Puddings

SERVES **6**

1 × 250g/9oz tin of sweetened chestnut purée

2 tablespoons Marsala

290ml/½ pint double cream

3 marrons glacés, thinly sliced

1. Stir the chestnut purée to break it up, then stir in the Marsala. Mix thoroughly.

2. Whip the cream until it just holds its shape and fold into the chestnut mixture with the marrons glacés.

3. Pour into 6 ramekins and chill thoroughly.

MARSALA

BLOODY MARY CRAB SALAD
(see page 18)

BAKED POUSSINS WITH
GARLIC AND LEMON
(see page 78)

MARRON GLACÉ PUDDINGS

Prune and Chocolate Puddings

SERVES 6

1 × 400g/14oz tin of prunes in syrup

3 tablespoons Armagnac or brandy

110g/4oz good-quality dark chocolate

15g/½oz butter

1 tablespoon water

450ml/¾ pint double cream

vanilla essence

1. Drain the prunes, reserving the syrup, and stone if necessary.

2. Put the prune syrup into a saucepan and reduce by boiling rapidly until very thick. Add the Armagnac and boil for 1 minute.

3. Melt the chocolate, butter and water together gently. Cool slightly until beginning to thicken.

4. Put the prunes and reduced syrup into a food processor and process until smooth.

5. Whip the cream until it just holds its shape and add the vanilla essence. Fold into the prune mixture and pour into a serving dish or 6 ramekins. Spread the chocolate mixture over the top and chill thoroughly.

AUSTRALIAN LIQUEUR MUSCAT

SMOKED HALIBUT WITH
JAPANESE-STYLE CUCUMBER
SALAD

(see page 39)

HONEY-GLAZED ROAST
PARTRIDGES

(see page 81)

PRUNE AND CHOCOLATE
PUDDINGS

Rhubarb Pots

SERVES 6

675g/1½lb rhubarb
1 orange
55g/2oz caster sugar
2 tablespoons orangeflower water
4 tablespoons dark brown sugar
150ml/5fl oz double cream
150ml/5fl oz Greek yoghurt

1. Cut the rhubarb into 2.5cm/1in pieces.

2. Pare one strip of orange zest with a vegetable peeler and grate the remainder finely.

3. Put the rhubarb into a saucepan with the strip of orange zest, caster sugar and orangeflower water. Cover the pan and stew very gently over a low heat until the rhubarb is almost tender.

4. Remove the rhubarb pieces and divide between 6 ramekins. Sprinkle over the grated orange zest and dark brown sugar.

5. Whip the cream lightly and fold in the yoghurt. Spoon over the rhubarb and refrigerate for at least 30 minutes.

ORANGE LIQUEUR

CHICORY SALAD WITH SMOKED
OYSTERS, PECANS AND
GORGONZOLA

(see page 17)

COLLOPS OF LAMB WITH
FLAGEOLET BEANS AND
OYSTER MUSHROOMS

(see page 97)

RHUBARB POTS

Passionfruit and Muscat Syllabub

SERVES 6

8 ripe passionfruits

*250ml/9fl oz good quality mascarpone cheese or
  cream cheese*

200ml/7fl oz crème fraîche

3 tablespoons Muscat wine

2 tablespoons icing sugar

juice of 1 lemon

1. Halve the passionfruits, scoop out the seeds and juice and set aside.

2. Mix together the mascarpone, crème fraîche and Muscat. Sift in the icing sugar. Season to taste with the lemon juice. Fold in the passionfruit seeds and juice, reserving a few seeds for decoration.

3. Pour into 6 stem glasses and decorate with the reserved seeds. Chill well before serving.

MUSCAT

SPINACH AND BACON SALAD WITH
RED CHILLI AND MANGO

(see page 20)

STIR-FRIED PRAWNS WITH
CORIANDER

(see page 57)

PASSIONFRUIT AND MUSCAT
SYLLABUB

Lemon Syllabub

SERVES 6

425ml/¾ pint double cream
finely grated zest of 1 lemon
juice of 3 lemons
3 tablespoons sweet white wine
icing sugar

TO DECORATE

thinly pared zest of 1 lemon

1. Place the cream in a bowl with the lemon zest. Whip, adding the lemon juice, wine and icing sugar at intervals, until the mixture just holds its shape. Spoon into individual glasses.

2. Cut the lemon zest into very thin needleshreds. Drop them into boiling water and cook for 2 minutes. Drain and dry on absorbent paper. Scatter on top of the syllabub.

MUSCAT DE BEAUMES DE VENISE

WARM CURRIED CHICKEN
LIVER SALAD
(see page 22)

SUN-DRIED AND CHERRY
TOMATO PASTA
(see page 123)

LEMON SYLLABUB

Ginger Syllabub

SERVES 6

6 tablespoons Advocaat liqueur
3 tablespoons ginger marmalade
425ml/¾ pint double cream

TO DECORATE

3 pieces of preserved ginger

1. Mix together the Advocaat and ginger marmalade.

2. Whip the cream lightly and stir in the marmalade mixture.

3. Spoon into small glasses, little china pots or coffee cups.

4. Put 2–3 thin slivers of preserved ginger on top of each syllabub. Chill before serving.

NOTE: For a smoother texture the ginger marmalade and the Advocaat can be liquidized or sieved together.

In the absence of ginger marmalade use orange marmalade well flavoured with finely chopped bottled ginger and its syrup.

AUSTRALIAN ORANGE MUSCAT

SWEET AND SPICY AUBERGINE
KEBABS
(see page 44)

GRILLED CHICKEN WITH MUSTARD
AND CRANBERRIES
(see page 72)

GINGER SYLLABUB

Lemon Curd Ice Cream

SERVES 6

6 egg yolks

finely grated zest and juice of 3 lemons

200g/7oz caster sugar

170g/6oz unsalted butter, at room temperature, cut
*   into small pieces*

860ml/1½ pints Greek yoghurt

1. Put the egg yolks, lemon juice, sugar and butter into a small saucepan. Put over a low heat and stir until the butter has melted and the curd coats the back of the spoon. Pass through a sieve. Add the lemon zest.

2. Allow the lemon curd to cool, then stir in the yoghurt. Cover closely and freeze.

3. Take the ice cream out of the freezer and put it into the refrigerator about 1 hour before serving.

NOTE: If time is very short you can use ready-made lemon curd.

SPARKLING SAUMUR

SPRING VEGETABLES IN
THAI-STYLE DRESSING
(see page 45)

SALMON PASTA WITH VERMOUTH
AND TARRAGON
(see page 125)

LEMON CURD ICE CREAM

Alain Senderens' Soupe aux Fruits Exotiques

This recipe was taken from Robert Carrier in the Sunday Express.

SERVES 6

2 small papayas
18 lychees
2 punnets of strawberries
3 kiwi fruits
8 passionfruits

FOR THE SYRUP

6 tablespoons sugar
1 sprig of mint
1 clove
¼ teaspoon Chinese five-spice powder
thinly pared zest of 1 lime
thinly pared zest of ¼ lemon
1 vanilla pod, split lengthwise
½ teaspoon peeled and finely chopped fresh root
   ginger
2 coriander seeds
450ml/¾ pint water

CRAB CAKES WITH HORSERADISH
RELISH

(see page 29)

CRACKED BLACK PEPPER PASTA
WITH TRUFFLE OIL
AND PARMESAN

(see page 114)

ALAIN SENDERENS' SOUPE AUX
FRUITS EXOTIQUES

TO DECORATE

1 tablespoon finely chopped mint

1. Make the syrup: put the sugar, sprig of mint, clove, Chinese five-spice, lime and lemon zest, vanilla pod, root ginger, coriander seeds and water into a heavy-bottomed saucepan. Bring slowly to the boil, stirring to dissolve the sugar. Reduce by boiling rapidly for 1 minute. Remove the pan from the heat and leave to infuse until cool.

2. Meanwhile, peel the papayas, scoop out the seeds and cut the flesh into even pieces. Skin the lychees and remove the stones. Wash and hull the strawberries. Peel the kiwi fruits and slice thinly.

3. When the syrup is cool, strain through a fine sieve into a bowl. Add the prepared fruits. Halve the passionfruits and scoop out the seeds and juice into the bowl of syrup. Chill for 2–3 hours.

4. To serve: divide the prepared fruits between 6 shallow bowls; spoon over the syrup and decorate with finely chopped mint.

GERMAN AUSLESE

Winter Fruit Salad

SERVES 6

675g/1½lb good-quality mixed dried fruits, such as
   prunes, apricots, figs, apples
2 tablespoons Calvados
cold tea
6 tablespoons fresh orange juice
5 cloves
5cm/2in piece of cinnamon stick
½ teaspoon ground mixed spice
pared zest of 1 lemon
1 star anise

1. Soak the mixed dried fruits in the Calvados and enough tea just to cover. Leave overnight.

2. Pour into a saucepan, add the orange juice, cloves, cinnamon, mixed spice, lemon zest and star anise. Bring to the boil, then reduce the heat and simmer until the fruits are soft. This will take about 20 minutes.

3. Remove and discard the cloves, cinnamon, lemon zest and star anise. Serve hot or cold.

MADEIRA

꒰

SPICED MUSHROOM BRUSCHETTA

(see page 49)

**SORREL, EGG AND ANCHOVY
PASTA**

(see page 126)

WINTER FRUIT SALAD

꒰

Roasted Coconut and Rum Cream

SERVES 6

30g/1oz desiccated sweetened coconut

110g/4oz creamed coconut, roughly chopped

4 tablespoons rum

400ml/14fl oz crème fraîche

finely grated zest of 1 lime

2–3 tablespoons icing sugar

1. Preheat the grill to its highest setting. Spread the desiccated coconut on a baking sheet and grill until golden-brown. Take care as the coconut browns very quickly.

2. Put the creamed coconut and rum into a small saucepan and heat gently to melt the coconut. Remove from the heat and leave to cool.

3. Fold the creamed coconut and rum into the crème fraîche. Add the lime zest and sift in icing sugar to taste.

4. Divide the mixture between 6 glasses, and refrigerate.

6. To serve: return to room temperature and sprinkle over the roasted coconut.

AMONTILLADO SHERRY

SPRING VEGETABLES IN
THAI-STYLE DRESSING

(see page 45)

GRILLED MACKEREL FILLETS
WITH CUCUMBER AND FENNEL
SALSA

(see page 62)

ROASTED COCONUT AND
RUM CREAM

CHEESE

by Juliet Harbutt

An integral part of French life, essential in Italian cuisine, and the backbone of the British sandwich, cheese is one of the most diverse and nutritious ingredients known to man, now available in a myriad of shapes, sizes and colours on the supermarket shelves and deli counters. Fortunately, distinguishing between the good and the bad, the mild and the vicious can be done with a little knowledge and a quick glance, a surreptitious sniff and perhaps a gentle squeeze because a cheese, unlike a book, can be judged by its rind or 'cover'. It is the moisture content of cheese that determines its texture, the type of rind it grows, its general characteristics and how it responds when cooked, and ultimately helps you create the ideal cheeseboard.

FRESH YOUNG CHEESES   Typically 1–10 days old, they have **no rind**, a delicate, lemony fresh flavour and just a hint of green pastures. When the rind is sticky or dull the cheese is past its best unless it is a French artisan goat's cheese, like crottin, ideal for grilling. These dry out and grow a **delicate bluish rind**.
Examples: Cream cheese, ricotta, fresh goat's cheese, mozzarella.
Cooking: Best used as spreads, dips, baked in pastries or lightly grilled. They will separate in sauces or when grilled under high heat except for the more dense mozzarella and crottin style.

BLOOMY RIND CHEESES   Covered in a **soft white rind** or **'bloom'** of penicillium, the immature interior is quite dry and chalky, becoming soft and, if thin like Brie, voluptuous and runny when ripe. They should smell of mushrooms, have soft not sharp edges and not be dry or cracked.
Examples: Camembert, Brie, Pavé d'Affinois, chèvre log, Somerset Brie, Chauvanne, Bonchester.
Cooking: Best used on the cheeseboard but can be breaded and deep-fried or cut off the rind and blended with cream cheese as a pâté.

SEMI-SOFT CHEESES   Washed or rubbed with salt to seal the rind, these develop either an **orangey/pink sticky rind** and a strong, pungent character, or, if left to ripen, they build up a **thin, leathery rind from orange to greyish-brown**, becoming mellow, supple, almost velvety. Some, like Edam, are waxed. The interior will discolour and the rind crack if poorly wrapped.
Examples: Edam, Munster, Port Salut, Chaumes, Gubbeens, St Davids, St Nectaire, raclette.
Cooking: the more mature ones grill superbly, holding their shape and releasing their lovely sweet, sour, fragrant aromas.

HARD CHEESES   Generally made in large rounds, they mature slowly, developing a full-bodied flavour and a **thick, dense rind often waxed or oiled**. From a firm supple texture and fruity tang like Gruyère to a hard yet still creamy nutty Cheddar through to Parmesan with its characteristic crumbly, almost grainy texture and delicious sweet, fruity yet pungent tang. Will split

and attract mould if poorly wrapped or too cold.
Examples: Cheddar, Cheshire, Parmesan, Gruyère, Wensleydale, Manchego, Pecorino.
Cooking: Ideal on cheeseboards and marvellous in sauces or grilled over vegetables, meat or fish, adding flavour and texture to traditional dishes across Europe.

BLUE CHEESES There are 2 types: those with a **soft white fuzzy rind** which behave like those mentioned above and those with rinds ranging from a **sticky white crust** to a **rough grey, almost gritty** texture, like Stilton. The blue is a penicillium mould encouraged to grow by piercing the cheese with rods (normally steel but can be wood or plastic). The blue mould then grows along the tunnel and cracks between the roughly packed curd. The blue veins must be evenly spread through the cheese.
Examples: Stilton, Roquefort, Cashel Blue, Gorgonzola.
Cooking: Wonderful on a cheeseboard and a little goes a long way when used in sauces, salads, soups or melted over pasta.

SPECIALITY CHEESES Made by adding flavourings like herbs, fruits or spices to well-known hard cheese.
Examples: White Stilton with Citrus, Cheddar with Date and Walnut, Wensleydale with Ginger.
Cooking: With so many fixed flavours they are generally best eaten as a dessert cheese after a meal though they do melt well in baked potatoes and sauces.

Buying and Serving Cheese

- A well-balanced cheeseboard should reflect different textures, as outlined above, as well as shapes, colours and milk types, eliminating the need for all but the most simple of garnishes – seasonal leaves, berries and maybe a few apples.
- Buy 1 or 2 wonderful chunks rather than lots of small pieces which dry out quickly and soon look unappetizing on a cheeseboard.
- Avoid serving strong fruits and vegetables like celery, citrus fruit, carrots and tomatoes with cheese, as they mask rather than enhance its flavour.
- Buy your cheeses ripe and eat them within a week or so. Do not expect Brie or Camembert to ripen in a cold refrigerator.
- Look out for the British Cheese Awards medals and the AOC label on French cheeses as these are symbols of excellence.
- Take cheese out of the refrigerator at least 1 hour before serving and allow to come to room temperature.
- Serve with bread: biscuits mask the unique texture of each cheese.

Storing Cheese

Soft, hard and blue cheeses should be wrapped in **wax paper**, or if you must use clingfilm make sure you leave a gap so the cheese can **breathe**. Then store the cheese in a larder, if you are lucky enough to have one, otherwise in a sealed **plastic box** in the refrigerator, preferably keeping blue and goat's separately.

Matching Wine and Cheese

As a general rule, the whiter the cheese, the whiter the accompanying wine should be, the darker more mature the cheese, the fuller and more robust the wine. Fruity reds tend to overpower, tannic wines need creamy Cheddar-type cheese to soften them. Blues and ewe's milk cheeses are enhanced by a crisp yet sweet white, and European cheeses marry well with wines from the same region. My favourite choice for a cheeseboard is Pinot Noir from Burgundy, Oregon or New Zealand. Its lovely soft, elegant flavours bring out the individuality of each cheese. Whatever you choose enjoy it, taste it, think of the effect it has on the texture and taste of the cheese and store it in your memory bank for next time.

Fresh Young Cheese

Wines: Fresh, crisp, fruity white wines like New Zealand Sauvignon Blanc or a Chenin bring out the delicate flavours of these cheeses.

Bloomy Rind Cheeses

Wines: Young cheeses with firm chalky centres are complemented well by Sauvignon Blancs and Pinot Grigio, but as they mature, developing a fuller, richer flavour and softer texture, a more rounded white is better, particularly a soft French Chardonnay. Very oaky Chardonnay with its characteristic tropical fruit flavour masks the subtle mushroomy character of the cheese.

Semi-Soft Cheeses

Wines: The pungent, sticky, orange-rinded cheeses need a spicy white like Gewürztraminer or a fruity red like Beaujolais. The more mellow grey crusted cheeses respond well to Merlot, Côtes du Ventoux and Pinot Noirs. Avoid wines with too much tannin.

Hard Cheeses

Wines: Caerphilly and the delicate goat's and ewe's milk cheeses need a soft red like Merlot or Savigny les Beaune. The complex, tangy character of a mature Cheddar, however, demands a red with real depth like the great Cabernet Sauvignons of Bordeaux, Australian Shiraz or even an Italian Barolo. Overly fruity reds are not appropriate.

Blue Cheeses

Wines: Port, contrary to traditional views, frequently dominates rather than marries with the wonderful spicy nature of these cheeses. Try a mellow old Port or Vintage Character or better still a crisp sweet pudding wine like a Late Harvest Muscat or a Barsac. The sweetness offsets the saltiness of the blues.

Speciality Cheeses

Wines: Difficult to generalize as they are made from so many different types of cheese and their added flavours can conflict with wine rather than enhance their individuality. As a basic rule the softer the cheese the lighter the wine, the harder the cheese the darker and richer the wine. Fruit likes fruit and those with herbs need a more delicate aromatic style.

BASIC RECIPES

PASTRY

When cooking in a hurry there will doubtless be many occasions when you haven't time to make your own pastry. However, as most home-made pastry tastes incomparably better than commercially prepared, and uncooked pastry freezes very well and can therefore be made well in advance, we have included a few pastry recipes.

Rich Shortcrust Pastry

170g/6oz plain flour
a pinch of salt
100g/3oz butter
1 egg yolk
very cold water

1. Sift the flour with the salt into a large bowl.
2. Rub in the butter until the mixture looks like coarse breadcrumbs.
3. Mix the egg yolk with 2 tablespoons water and add to the mixture.
4. Mix to a firm dough, first with a knife, and finally with one hand. It may be necessary to add more water, but the pastry should not be too damp. (Though crumbly pastry is more difficult to handle, it produces a shorter, lighter result.)
5. Chill, wrapped, for 30 minutes before using, or allow to relax after rolling out but before baking.

NOTE: For flavoured savoury pastry, add chopped thyme, poppy seeds, crushed caraway seeds.
To make sweet rich shortcrust pastry, mix in 1 tablespoon caster sugar once the fat has been rubbed into the flour.

Sweet Pastry

170g/6oz plain flour
a large pinch of salt
½ teaspoon baking powder
100g/3½oz unsalted butter
55g/2oz caster sugar
1 egg yolk
55ml/2fl oz double cream

1. Sift the flour, salt and baking powder into a large bowl.
2. Rub in the butter until the mixture looks like coarse breadcrumbs. Stir in the sugar.
3. Mix the egg yolk with the cream and add to the mixture.
4. Mix to a firm dough, first with a knife, and finally with one hand. Chill, wrapped, for 30 minutes before using, or allow to relax after rolling out but before baking.

NOTE: For flavoured sweet pastry, add finely grated orange or lemon zest, or ground cinnamon.

Pâte Sucrée

170g/6oz plain flour
a pinch of salt
85g/3oz butter, softened
3 egg yolks
85g/3oz sugar
2 drops of vanilla essence

1. Sift the flour on to a board with a pinch of salt. Make a large well in the centre and put the butter in it. Place the egg yolks and sugar on the butter with the vanilla essence.

2. Using the fingertips of one hand, mix the butter, yolks and sugar together. When mixed to a soft paste, draw in the flour and knead until the pastry is just smooth.

3. If the pastry is very soft, chill before rolling or pressing out to the required shape. In any event the pastry must be allowed to relax for 30 minutes either before or after rolling out, but before baking.

Rough Puff Pastry

225g/8oz plain flour
a pinch of salt
140g/5oz butter
very cold water

1. Sift the flour and salt into a cold bowl. Cut the butter into knobs about the size of a sugar lump and add to the flour. Do not rub in but add enough water just to bind the paste together. Mix first with a knife, then with one hand. Knead very lightly.

2. Wrap the pastry in clingfilm or a cloth and leave to relax for 10 minutes in the refrigerator.

3. On a floured board, roll the pastry into a strip about 30 × 10cm/12 × 4in long. This must be done carefully, with a heavy rolling pin: press firmly on the pastry and give short sharp rolls until the pastry has reached the required size. The surface of the pastry should not be over-stretched and broken.

4. Fold the strip into 3 and turn so that the folded edge is to your left, like a closed book.

5. Again roll out into a strip 1cm/½in thick. Fold in 3 again and leave, wrapped, in the refrigerator for 15 minutes.

6. Roll and fold the pastry as before, then chill again for 15 minutes.

7. Roll and fold again, by which time the pastry should be ready for use, with no signs of streakiness.

8. Roll into the required shape.

9. Chill again before baking.

Puff Pastry

225g/8oz plain flour
a pinch of salt
30g/1oz lard
150ml/5fl oz icy water
140–200g/5–7oz butter

1. If you have never made puff pastry before, use the smaller amount of butter: this will give a normal pastry. If you have some experience, more butter will produce a lighter, very rich pastry.
2. Sift the flour with a pinch of salt into a large bowl. Rub in the lard. Add the water and mix with a knife to a doughy consistency. Turn on to the work top and knead quickly until just smooth. Wrap in clingfilm or a cloth and leave to relax in the refrigerator for 30 minutes.
3. Lightly flour the work top or board and roll the dough into a rectangle about 10 × 30cm/4 × 12in long.
4. Tap the butter lightly with a floured rolling pin to get it into a flattened block about 9 × 8cm/ 3½ × 3in. Put the butter on to the rectangle of pastry and fold both ends over to enclose it. Fold the third closest to you over first and then bring the top third down. Press the sides together to prevent the butter escaping. Give it a 90-degree anti-clockwise turn so that the folded, closed edge is on your left.
5. Now tap the pastry parcel with the rolling pin to flatten the butter a little; then roll out, quickly and lightly, until the pastry is 3 times as long as it is wide. Fold it very evenly in 3, first folding the third closest to you over, then bringing the top third down. Give it a 90-degree anti-clockwise turn so that the folded, closed edge is on your left.

Again press the edges firmly with the rolling pin. Then roll out again to form a rectangle as before.
6. Now the pastry has had 2 rolls and folds, or 'turns' as they are called. It should be put to rest in a cool place for 30 minutes or so. The rolling and folding must be repeated twice more, the pastry again rested, and then again given 2 more 'turns'. This makes a total of 6 turns. If the butter is still very streaky, roll and fold it once more.

*

Melba Toast

6 slices white bread

1. Preheat the grill to its highest setting. Preheat the oven to 150°C/300°F/gas mark 2.
2. Grill the bread on both sides until well browned.
3. While still hot, quickly cut off the crusts and split each slice in half horizontally.
4. Arrange the bread slices, toasted side down, on a baking sheet.
5. Put the toast in the oven and leave until dry and brittle.

NOTE: Melba toast can be kept for a day or two in an airtight tin but it will lose its flavour if kept longer, and is undoubtedly best served straight from the oven.

STOCKS AND SAVOURY SAUCES

Larousse *Dictionnaire Gastronomique* defines a sauce as a 'liquid seasoning for food', and this covers anything from juices in a frying pan to complicated and sophisticated emulsions. Most of the recipes in this book incorporate simple sauces as and when necessary. We have, however, included in this section a few of the classic sauces as well as some that are quick and easy.

Behind many a great soup or sauce stands a good stock. Stock is flavoured liquid, and the basic flavour can be fish, poultry, meat or vegetable. Stocks can take a long time to make, but they can be made well in advance and frozen very successfully. Before freezing, strain the stock and skim off all the fat. Reduce by boiling rapidly until syrupy, skimming frequently as it boils. Freeze the resulting 'glace' in ice-cube trays and then turn the frozen cubes into a tightly sealed freezer. They will keep in the freezer for at least a year.

If you have no stock available we recommend avoiding the use of stock cubes. Many supermarkets now produce fresh stock in tubs, but water is often a perfectly suitable substitute (as in Roast Sweet Pepper Soup, for example, see page 8).

Beef Stock

900g/2lb beef bones
1 onion, peeled and chopped, skin reserved
2 carrots, roughly chopped
1 tablespoon oil
parsley stalks
2 bay leaves
6 black peppercorns

1. Preheat the oven to 220°C/425°F/gas mark 7.
2. Put the beef bones into a roasting tin and brown in the oven. This may take up to 1 hour.
3. Brown the onions and carrots in the oil in a large stock pot. It is essential that they do not burn.

4. When the bones are well browned, add them to the vegetables with the onion skins, parsley stalks, bay leaves and peppercorns. Cover with cold water and bring very slowly to the boil, skimming off any scum as it rises to the surface.
5. When clear of scum, simmer gently for 3–4 hours, or even longer, skimming off the fat as necessary and topping up with water if the level gets very low. The longer it simmers, and the more the liquid reduces by evaporation, the stronger the stock will be.
6. Strain, cool and lift off any remaining fat.

Chicken Stock

onion, sliced
celery, sliced
carrot, sliced
chicken or veal bones, skin or flesh
parsley
thyme
bay leaf
black peppercorns

1. Put all the ingredients into a saucepan. Cover generously with cold water and bring to the boil slowly. Skim off any fat, and/or scum.
2. Simmer for 2–3 hours, skimming frequently and topping up the water level if necessary. The liquid should reduce to half the original quantity.
3. Strain, cool and lift off all the fat.

Glace de Viande

570ml/1 pint beef stock (see page 184), absolutely
   free of fat.

1. In a heavy-bottomed saucepan reduce the brown stock by boiling over a steady heat until thick and clear.
2. Pour into small pots. When cold cover with polythene or jam covers and secure.
3. Keep in the refrigerator until ready for use.

NOTE: Keeps for several weeks in freezer and is very useful for enriching sauces.

Fish Stock

onion, sliced
carrot, sliced
celery, sliced
fish bones, skins, fins, heads or tails, crustacean
   shells (such as prawn shells, mussel shells, etc.)
parsley stalks
bay leaf
a pinch of chopped thyme
black peppercorns

1. Put all the ingredients into a saucepan, with cold water to cover, and bring to the boil. Reduce the heat to a simmer and skim off any scum.
2. Simmer for 20 minutes if the fish bones are small, 30 minutes if large. Strain.

NOTE: The flavour of fish stock is impaired if the bones are cooked for too long. Once strained, however, it may be strengthened by further boiling and reducing.

Fish Glaze

Fish glaze (*glace de poisson*) is simply very well-reduced, very well strained fish stock, which is used to flavour and enhance fish sauces. It can be kept refrigerated for about 3 days or frozen in ice cube trays and used as required.

Court Bouillon

1 litre/2 pints water
150ml/5fl oz white wine vinegar
1 carrot, sliced
1 onion, sliced
1 stick of celery
12 black peppercorns
2 bay leaves
2 tablespoons salad oil
salt

1. Bring all the ingredients to the boil in a saucepan, then simmer for 20 minutes.
2. Allow the liquid to cool and place the fish, meat or vegetables in it, then bring slowly to simmering point.

Vegetable Stock

4 tablespoons oil
1 onion, roughly chopped
1 leek, roughly chopped
1 large carrot, roughly chopped
2 sticks of celery, roughly chopped
a few cabbage leaves, roughly shredded
a few mushroom stalks
2 cloves of garlic, crushed
a few parsley stalks
6 black peppercorns
sea salt
1 large bay leaf
6 tablespoons dry white wine
570ml/1 pint water

1. Heat the oil in a large saucepan. Add the vegetables, garlic and parsley, cover and cook gently for 5 minutes or until softening.
2. Add the peppercorns, salt, bay leaf, wine and water and bring to the boil. Reduce the heat and simmer for 30 minutes or until the liquid is reduced by half.
3. Strain the stock through a sieve, pressing hard to remove as much of the liquid as possible. Discard the vegetable pulp. Allow to cool and skim off any fat.
4. Use as required.

White Sauce

This is a quick and easy basic white sauce.

20g/¾oz butter
20g/¾oz flour
a pinch of dry English mustard
290ml/½ pint creamy milk
salt and freshly ground white pepper

1. Melt the butter in a thick-bottomed saucepan.
2. Add the flour and the mustard and stir over the heat for 1 minute. Remove the pan from the heat, pour in the milk and mix well.
3. Return the sauce to the heat and stir constantly until boiling.
4. Simmer for 2–3 minutes and season to taste with salt and pepper.

NOTE: Various flavourings may be added, such as 1 tablespoon chopped parsley or 2 tablespoons chopped watercress.

Mornay Sauce (Cheese Sauce)

20g/¾oz butter
20g/¾oz flour
a pinch of dry English mustard
a pinch of cayenne pepper
290ml/½ pint milk
55g/2oz Gruyère or strong Cheddar cheese, grated
15g/½oz Parmesan cheese, freshly grated
salt and freshly ground black pepper

1. Melt the butter in a heavy-bottomed saucepan and stir in the flour, mustard and cayenne pepper. Cook, stirring, for 1 minute. Remove the pan from the heat. Pour in the milk and mix well.
2. Return the pan to the heat and stir until boiling. Simmer, stirring well, for 2 minutes.
3. Add all the cheese, and mix well, but do not reboil.
4. Season to taste with salt and pepper.

Blender Hollandaise

3 tablespoons white wine vinegar
6 black peppercorns
1 bay leaf
1 blade of mace
110g/4oz unsalted butter
2 egg yolks
salt
lemon juice

1. Put the vinegar, peppercorns, bay leaf and mace into a small, heavy saucepan and reduce by simmering to 1 tablespoon. Strain and reserve.
2. Melt the butter and keep hot. Put the egg yolks into a liquidizer with the reduced vinegar and a pinch of salt and, with the motor still running, add the melted butter in a slow, steady stream. Season to taste with lemon juice, salt and pepper. Pour into a warm bowl standing in hot water, to keep warm.

Mayonnaise

2 egg yolks
salt and freshly ground white pepper
1 teaspoon Dijon mustard
290ml/½ pint olive oil, or 150ml/5fl oz each olive
    and salad oil
a squeeze of lemon juice
1 tablespoon white wine vinegar

1. Put the egg yolks into a bowl with a pinch of salt and the mustard and beat well with a wooden spoon.
2. Add the oil, literally drop by drop, beating all the time. The mixture should be very thick by the time half the oil is added.
3. Beat in the lemon juice.
4. Resume pouring in the oil, going rather more confidently now, but alternating the dribbles of oil with small quantities of vinegar.
5. Season to taste with salt and pepper.

NOTE: If the mixture curdles, see note on page 189.

Blender Mayonnaise

2 eggs

1 teaspoon Dijon mustard

salt and freshly ground white pepper

290ml/½ pint olive oil, or 150ml/5fl oz each olive
*   oil and salad oil*

juice of 1 lemon

1. Put the eggs and mustard with a pinch of salt
into a liquidizer and whizz briefly.

2. Add the oil, with the motor still running, in a
slow, steady stream. The mixture should be very
thick by the time half the oil is added.

3. Add lemon juice to taste and continue pouring
in the oil. Season to taste with salt and pepper.

NOTE: If the mixture curdles, add 1 tablespoon
water and whizz. If this fails, pour the curdled
mixture into a bowl, put another egg into the
liquidizer and very slowly add the curdled
mixture.

Beurre Blanc

225g/8oz unsalted butter

1 tablespoon chopped shallot

3 tablespoons white wine vinegar

3 tablespoons water

salt and freshly ground white pepper

a squeeze of lemon juice

1. Chill the butter, then cut it into 3 lengthwise,
then across into thin slices. Keep cold.

2. Put the shallot, vinegar and water into a thick-
bottomed sauté pan or small shallow saucepan.
Boil to reduce to about 2 tablespoons. Strain and
return to the pan.

3. Lower the heat under the pan. Using a wire
whisk and plenty of vigorous continuous
whisking, gradually add the butter, piece by piece.
The process should take about 5 minutes and the
sauce should become thick, creamy and pale –
rather like a thin Hollandaise. Season to taste with
salt, pepper and lemon juice.

For variations on these sauces see page 190.

Mayonnaise, Hollandaise and Beurre Blanc Variations

Add any of these flavourings after the sauce has been made:

- Roasted garlic; chopped watercress; chopped sorrel; chopped capers; chopped gherkins; deseeded and chopped red or green chilli.
- Chopped herbs: chives; dill; chervil; basil; parsley; tarragon.
- Red or green pesto; sundried tomato paste; green or black tapenade; rocket paste; anchovy paste, artichoke paste, horseradish relish.

French Dressing

6 tablespoons olive oil
2 tablespoons wine vinegar
salt and freshly ground black pepper

1. Put all the ingredients into a screw-top jar.
2. Before using shake until well emulsified.

NOTE: If kept in the refrigerator, the dressing will form an emulsion more easily when whisked or shaken, and has a slightly thicker consistency.

French Dressing Variations

- **Oils**

  Olive; sunflower; peanut/arachide; grapeseed; walnut; hazelnut; sesame (use 50:50 with plain oil); truffle; chilli (use very sparingly, 1 teaspoon to 3 tablespoons plain oil)

- **Vinegars**

  White wine; red wine; cider; sherry; champagne; rice wine vinegar

  Balsamic

  Flavoured vinegars: tarragon; basil; rosemary; raspberry

  Honeygar (available from health food shops)

  Citrus juices: lemon; lime; grapefruit

- **Mustards**

  English; Dijon; grainy or any flavoured mustard

- **Nuts, Spices and Seeds**

  Toasted chopped walnuts; hazelnuts; pecans; macadamias; almonds; pinenuts

- Toasted ground cumin; Chinese five-spice powder; toasted ground Sichuan peppercorns

- Poppy; sesame; toasted caraway; pumpkin; sunflower

- **Chopped herbs**

  Tarragon; parsley; basil; chervil; coriander; thyme; chives; dill; mint; fennel fronds

- **Dairy**

  Roquefort; feta; Parmesan; fromage frais, crème fraîche

- **Vegetables**

  Roasted garlic, puréed; chopped spring onions; chopped shallots; chopped red onion; chopped truffles; chopped fresh chilli

Easy Tomato Sauce

1 × 400g/14oz tin of plum tomatoes

1 small onion, chopped

1 small carrot, chopped

1 stick of celery, chopped

½ clove of garlic, crushed

1 bay leaf

parsley stalks

salt and freshly ground black pepper

juice of ½ lemon

a dash of Worcestershire sauce (optional)

1 teaspoon sugar

1 teaspoon chopped basil or thyme

1. Put all the ingredients into a thick-bottomed saucepan, cover and simmer over a medium heat for 30 minutes.

2. Pour into a liquidizer or food processor and process until smooth, then push through a sieve.

3. Return the sauce to the pan. If the sauce is too thin, reduce by boiling rapidly. Check the seasoning, adding more salt or sugar if necessary.

Pesto Sauce

2 cloves of garlic, peeled
2 large cups of basil leaves
55g/2oz pinenuts
55g/2oz Parmesan cheese, freshly grated
150ml/5fl oz olive oil
salt and freshly ground black pepper

1. Put the garlic and basil into a liquidizer and whizz to a paste.
2. Add the nuts and cheese, then, with the motor still running, slowly pour in the oil through the feed hole in the lid. Season to taste with salt and pepper.
3. Keep in a covered jar in a cool place.

NOTE: Pesto is sometimes made with walnuts instead of pinenuts, and the nuts may be pounded with the other ingredients to give a smooth paste. If the sauce is in danger of curdling, add 1 tablespoon warm water and mix again.
Pesto sauce can be kept in the refrigerator for 2–3 weeks.

Parsley Pesto

2 cloves of garlic
1 large handful of parsley, roughly chopped
30g/1oz blanched almonds
150ml/5fl oz good-quality olive oil
55g/2oz Cheddar cheese, finely grated

1. Put the garlic and parsley into a liquidizer and whizz to a paste.
2. Mix in the nuts, then, with the motor still running, slowly pour in the oil through the feed hole in the lid.
3. Quickly mix in the cheese.
4. Keep in a covered jar in a cool place.

NOTE: If the pesto is in danger of curdling, add 1 tablespoon warm water and mix again.
The pesto can be kept in the refrigerator for 2–3 weeks.
For Coriander Pesto see page 31.

Mushroom Sauce

handfuls of mixed herbs (tarragon, parsley, chervil)
150ml/5fl oz chicken stock (see page 185)
220ml/8fl oz double cream
30g/1oz butter
110g/4oz button mushrooms, chopped
110g/4oz oyster mushrooms, sliced
salt and freshly ground black pepper

1. Drop the herbs into a saucepan of boiling salted water. Bring back to the boil, then strain through a sieve. Pour cold water on to the herbs and squeeze out any excess moisture. Put into a liquidizer.
2. Put the stock and cream into a saucepan and bring to the boil, then reduce the heat and simmer until a coating consistency is achieved. Pour into the liquidizer and whizz with the herbs until smooth and green.
3. Melt the butter in a sauté pan, add the mushrooms and cook until soft and any liquid has evaporated. Add the herb sauce to the pan and reheat. Season to taste with salt and pepper.

Tomato, Basil and Olive Oil Sauce

55ml/2fl oz olive oil
1 clove of garlic, flattened but not crushed
2 medium tomatoes, peeled, deseeded and finely
* chopped*
4 large basil leaves
salt and freshly ground black pepper

1. Put the oil and garlic into a small saucepan and place over a low heat to infuse for a few minutes.
2. Remove the garlic and add the tomatoes and basil. Season to taste with salt and pepper.
3. Serve warm.

Thick Onion and Mint Sauce

1 large Spanish onion, very finely chopped
55g/2oz butter
3 tablespoons water
2 tablespoons chopped mint
salt and freshly ground black pepper

1. Cook the onion slowly in the butter and water until very soft but not coloured. Push through a sieve, or whizz in a liquidizer.
2. Mix in the mint and season to taste with salt and pepper.

Cumberland Sauce

2 oranges
1 lemon
225g/8oz redcurrant jelly
1 shallot, chopped
150ml/5fl oz port or red wine
½ teaspoon Dijon mustard
a pinch of cayenne pepper
a pinch of ground ginger

1. Peel 1 orange and the lemon, removing only the outer skin. Cut the zest into fine shreds.
2. Squeeze the fruit juice and strain into a pan. Then add the remaining ingredients with the shredded zest. Simmer for 10 minutes, then cool.

Apple Sauce

450g/1lb cooking apples
finely grated zest of ¼ lemon
3 tablespoons water
2 teaspoons sugar
15g/½oz butter

1. Peel, quarter, core and slice the apples.
2. Place in a heavy saucepan with the lemon zest, water and sugar. Cover and cook over a very low heat until the apples are soft.
3. Beat in the butter, allow to cool slightly and add extra sugar if required. Serve hot or cold.

Mint Sauce

a large handful of fresh mint
2 tablespoons caster sugar
2 tablespoons hot water
2 tablespoons vinegar

1. Wash the mint and shake dry. Remove the stalks, and chop the leaves finely. Place in a bowl with the sugar.
2. Pour on the water and leave for 5 minutes until the sugar has dissolved. Add the vinegar and leave to soak for 1–2 hours.

Walnut and Parsley Sauce

30g/1oz walnuts
1 bunch of parsley, roughly chopped
1 clove of garlic, peeled
290ml/½ pint single cream
30g/1oz Parmesan cheese, freshly grated
salt and freshly ground black pepper

1. Put the walnuts, parsley and garlic into a food processor and process until finely chopped. Transfer to a bowl.
2. Stir in the cream and Parmesan cheese (do not process again), season to taste with salt and pepper.

Tomato and Mint Salsa

1 shallot, finely diced

1 tablespoon red wine vinegar

3 tablespoons extra virgin olive oil

4 tomatoes, peeled, deseeded and finely chopped

1 tablespoon chopped mint

salt and freshly ground black pepper

1. Mix together the shallot, vinegar and oil and allow to stand for 10 minutes.

2. Add the tomatoes and mint and season to taste with salt and pepper.

Pineapple and Coriander Salsa

1 small pineapple, peeled and cored

1 tablespoon groundnut oil

1 small red onion, very finely chopped

1cm/½in piece of fresh root ginger, peeled and very finely chopped

½ tablespoon cider vinegar

4 tablespoons chopped coriander

salt and freshly ground black pepper

1. Cut the pineapple into small chunks and set aside.

2. Heat the oil in a large frying pan, add the onion and ginger and sweat until soft but not coloured.

3. Add the pineapple and vinegar and warm through. Add the coriander and season to taste with salt and pepper.

SWEET SAUCES

Crème Chantilly

150ml/5fl oz double cream
2 tablespoons iced water
1 teaspoon icing sugar
2 drops of vanilla essence

1. Put all the ingredients into a chilled bowl and whisk with a balloon whisk, steadily but not too fast, for about 2 minutes or until the cream has thickened and doubled in volume.
2. Whisk faster for 30–40 seconds until the mixture is very fluffy and will form soft peaks.

NOTE: Chilling the ingredients and the bowl gives a lighter, whiter result.

Crème Anglaise (English Egg Custard)

290ml/½ pint milk
1 tablespoon sugar
1 vanilla pod or a few drops of vanilla essence
2 egg yolks

1. Heat the milk and vanilla pod in a thick-bottomed saucepan and bring slowly to the boil.
2. Beat the yolks with the sugar in a bowl. Remove the vanilla pod and pour the milk on to the egg yolks, stirring steadily. Mix well and return to the pan.
3. Stir over a low heat for about 5 minutes or until the mixture thickens so that it will coat the back of a spoon. Do not boil. Pour into a cold bowl.
4. Add the vanilla essence, if used.

Orange Crème Anglaise

570ml/1 pint milk
finely grated zest of 1 orange
1 vanilla pod
85g/3oz sugar
6 egg yolks
2 tablespoons Grand Marnier
1 drop of orange essence

1. Heat the milk with the orange zest and vanilla pod and bring slowly to the boil. Turn off the heat and leave to infuse for 10 minutes.
2. Beat the sugar and egg yolks together. Pour the milk on to the mixture, stirring steadily. Remove the vanilla pod.
3. Return the milk to the pan and cook over a low heat, stirring well, for about 5 minutes or until the mixture thickens and will coat the back of a spoon.
4. Strain into a bowl and add the Grand Marnier and orange essence. Allow to cool before using.

Mocha Custard

570ml/1 pint milk
16 coffee beans
100g/4oz plain chocolate
4 egg yolks
30g/1oz caster sugar

1. Put the milk into a small saucepan with the coffee beans. Place over a low heat and bring to the boil. Turn off the heat and leave to infuse for 10 minutes.
2. Break the chocolate into small even pieces and put them into a heatproof bowl over (not in) a saucepan of simmering water. Allow to melt completely.
3. Beat the egg yolks with the sugar.
4. Strain the milk into the bowl of melted chocolate and add to the egg-yolk mixture.
5. Pour this mixture into a rinsed out thick-bottomed saucepan and stir steadily over a medium heat for 3–4 minutes or until the mixture thickens so that it will coat the back of a spoon. Do not boil. Allow to cool before using.

Caramel Sauce

225g/8oz granulated sugar
290ml/½ pint water

1. Put the sugar into a thick-bottomed saucepan with half the water.
2. Dissolve the sugar slowly without stirring or allowing the water to boil.
3. Once all the sugar has dissolved turn up the heat and boil until it is a good caramel colour.
4. Immediately tip in the remaining water (it will fizz dangerously, so stand back).
5. Stir until any lumps have dissolved, then remove from the heat and allow to cool.

Toffee Sauce

2 tablespoons brandy (optional)
110g/4oz butter
55g/2oz demerara sugar
2 tablespoons double cream

1. Put all the ingredients into a thick-bottomed saucepan and heat until melted.
2. Bring to the boil and allow to thicken slightly. Allow to cool.

Apricot Sauce

110g/4oz dried apricots, soaked overnight
110g/4oz tinned apricots
570ml/1 pint water

1. Drain the dried apricots and put them into a saucepan with the tinned apricots and water. Bring to the boil, then reduce the heat and simmer until tender.
2. Liquidize, then push through a sieve. If the sauce is too thin, reduce it by boiling rapidly to the required consistency. If it is too thick, add a little water.

NOTE: This sauce can be served hot or cold.

Fruit Preserves Sauce

85g/3oz granulated sugar
150ml/5fl oz water
3 tablespoons good-quality fruit preserves

1. Put the sugar and water into a saucepan and heat slowly until the sugar has dissolved. Boil rapidly until the syrup feels tacky between finger and thumb.
2. Add the jam and stir until completely melted. Sieve to remove any pips or skin.

Flavoured Butters

Use on pancakes, waffles or mince pies.

225g/8oz unsalted butter, softened
225g/8oz icing sugar, sifted
finely grated zest of 1 orange, lemon or lime
(optional)
4 tablespoons any liqueur or spirit

1. Cream the butter and sugar until very light.
2. Add the citrus zest, if used, and the liqueur or spirit to flavour fairly strongly. Serve well chilled.

Mango Coulis

2 mangoes, peeled, stoned and cut into large
chunks
juice of ½ lemon
icing sugar

1. Whizz the mangoes in a liquidizer or food processor with the lemon juice until smooth.
2. Push through a sieve and sift in icing sugar to taste.

Yoghurt and Lemon Curd Sauce

1 × 450g/1lb jar good-quality lemon curd or cheese
570ml/1 pint Greek yoghurt
finely grated zest of 1 lemon

1. Mix the lemon curd or cheese and yoghurt together with the lemon zest.
2. Chill thoroughly before serving.

Easy Chocolate Sauce

30g/1oz butter
100ml/3½fl oz milk
55g/2oz cocoa powder
170g/6oz icing sugar
vanilla essence

1. Melt the butter in the milk in a saucepan over a low heat, sift in the cocoa powder and icing sugar and stir thoroughly until they have dissolved.
2. Add a few drops of vanilla essence to taste.

Butterscotch Sauce

110g/4oz soft brown syrup
110g/4oz golden syrup
110g/4oz butter
vanilla essence

1. Put the sugar, syrup and butter into a thick-bottomed saucepan and bring to the boil slowly, stirring constantly, until the sugar has dissolved.
2. Add vanilla essence to taste.

SUPPLIERS

Meat, Poultry, Game, Charcuterie, Smoked Food and Seafood

Fletchers of Auchtermuchty

Reediehill Farm

Auchtermuchty

Fife KY14 7HS

Tel: 01337 828369

Fresh vacuum-packed oven-ready venison. All cuts available.

Goodmans Geese

Walsgrove Farm

Great Witley

Worcester

WR6 6JJ

Tel: 01299 896272

Oven-ready geese available from Michaelmas to Christmas.

Heal Farm Meats

Kingsnympton

Umberleigh

Devon EX37 9TB

Tel: 01769 574341

Additive-free meats and game. Wonderful sausages, hams and pâtés. Special recipes for restricted diets. All can be smoked on request.

Heritage Foods

Lakeside

Bridgewater Road

Barrow Gurney

Bristol

Avon BS19 1BA

Tel: 01275 474707

Specialists in wild and chemical-free salmon – can get any fish delivered the following day.

Leathams Larder

114 Camberwell Road

London SE5 0EE

Tel: 0171 703 7031

Charcuterie, delicatessen, game, fish, seafood, poultry and specialist provisions.

C. Lidgate

110 Holland Park Avenue

London W11 4UA

Tel: 0171 727 8243

Family butcher specializing in high-quality meat, sausages and pâtés.

Inverawe Smokehouses

Inverawe

Taynuilt

Argyll PA35 1HU

Tel: 0186 6822 446

Traditionally smoked meat, game, fish and cheese.

Derek Fox

25 Market Place

Malton

North Yorkshire YO17 0LP

Tel: 0653 600338

Additive-free meat and game, sausages, hams and pâtés.

Marney Meats

Layer Marney Tower, Layer Marney, Colchester,

Essex CO5 9US

Tel: 01206 330784

Kid, venison, pork lamb and beef: legs, long loins and diced shoulder.

Naturally Yours

The Horse and Gate, Witcham Toll, Ely,

Cambridgeshire CB6 2AB

Tel: 01353 778725

Rare breeds: beef, mutton, lamb, pork, bacon, game and sausages.

Kelly Turkey Farms

Springate Farm, Bicknacre Road, Danbury, Essex

CM3 4EP

Tel: 01245 223581

Cambridge Bronze turkeys, a breed with superb flavour and texture.

W. E. Botterill & Son

Lings View Farm, Croxton Kerrial, Grantham,

Lincolnshire NG32 1QP

Tel: 01476 870394

Freerange geese and turkeys.

Swaddles Green Farm

Hare Lane, Buckland St Mary, Chard, Somerset

TA20 3JR

Tel: 01460 234387

Organic meat: lamb, pork, poultry and beef.

Real Meat Co Ltd

East Hill Farm

Heytesbury

Warminster

Wiltshire BA12 0H

Tel: 01985 840436

Full range of meat, poultry and bacon all reared without growth promoters.

Oriental Specialist Ingredients

Hong's Chinese Supermarket

7A Bath Street, Glasgow G2 1HY

Tel: 0141 332 4492

Steamboat Oriental Foods

P.O. Box 452, Bradford, West Yorkshire BD4 7TF

(no phone no.)

Thai, Indian, Pakistani, Chinese and Japanese foods.

Wing Yip

395 Edgware Road, London NW2 6IW

Tel: 0181 450 0422

Japanese, Chinese and Thai foods.

Yaohan Plaza

399 Edgware Road, Colindale, London NW9 0JJ

Tel: 0181 200 0009

All types of fresh and canned Japanese foods.

Fox's Spices

Masons Road, Stratford-upon-Avon, Warwickshire
CV37 9NF
Tel: 01789 266420
Spices, herbs, mustards, peppers and oriental spices.

Fiddes Payne Herbs and Spices Ltd

The Spice Warehouse, Pepper Alley, Banbury,
Oxfordshire OX16 8JB
Tel: 012295 253888
Herbs and spices in all forms and essential oils.

Julian Graves Ltd

Oakdate Trading Estate, Ham Lane, off Stalling
Lane, Kingswinford, West Midlands DY6 73H
Tel: 01384 277772
Dried exotic fruits.

L'Aquila

40 Caledonian Road, King's Cross, London N1 9DT
Tel: 0171 837 5555
Truffles, dried mushrooms and saffron.

Lina's

18 Brewer Street, London W1
Tel: 0171 437 6482
Home-made pasta, beans, olives, Italian breads,
pastries, salamis, cheeses, dried mushrooms.

Taylor & Lake

44/54 Stewarts Road, London SW8 4DF
Tel: 0171 622 9156
Salted capers, sun-dried tomatoes, fine oils and
specialist Mediterranean foods.

Wild Oats

210 Westbourne Grove, London W11 2RH
Tel: 0171 229 1063
Health food shop; organic foods.

Chocolates

Green & Blacks

Unit 112
Canalot Studios
222 Kensal Road
London W10 5BN
Tel: 0181 970 9679

Melchior Chocolates

Tinto House
Station Road
South Molton
Devon EX36 3LL
Tel: 01769 574442
A range of over 40 flavoured truffles and pralines.

Chocolate Society

Norwood Bottom Farm
Ottley
Near Leeds
West Yorkshire LS21 2RH
Tel: 0943 851101
Suppliers of block couverture, handmade chocolate
and specialist cook's ingredients.

Cheese

Chewton Dairy Farms
Priory Farm
Chewton Mendip
Somerset BA3 4NT
Tel: 01761 241666
Traditional Cheddar cheese packed any size.

Comestibles
82 Bailgate, Lincoln, Lincolnshire
Tel: 01522 520010

The Fine Cheese Co
29 Walcot Street, Bath, Avon
Tel: 01225 483407

Godfrey C. Williams & Sons
9–11 The Square, Sandbach, Cheshire
Tel: 01270 762817

Iain Mellis The Cheesemonger
30a Victoria Street, Edinburgh
Tel: 0131 226 6215

Irma Fingal Rock
64 Monnow Street, Monmouth, Gwent
Tel: 01600 712372

Jeroboams
24 Bute Street, London SW7
Tel: 0171 225 2232
1 Elizabeth Street
London SW1
Tel: 0171 727 9359
6 Clarendon Road
London W11
Tel: 0171 727 9359

Neal's Yard Dairy
17 Shorts Gardens, London WC2
Tel: 0171 379 7646
Mail order.

Oxford Cheese Company
17 The Covered Market, Market Street, Oxford,
Oxfordshire
Tel: 01865 721420

Paxton & Whitfield
Head office: call for branches.
13 Wood Street, Stratford-upon-Avon,
Warwickshire
Tel: 01789 415544

Ticklemore Cheese Shop
1 Ticklemore Street, Totnes, Devon
Tel: 01803 865926

Cream and Ice Cream

Childhay Manor Dairy

Crewkerne Business Park

Blacknell Lane

Crewkerne

Somerset TA18 7HJ

Tel: 01460 77422

Dairy ice cream. No additives or artificial colourings. Will make up to customer's own flavours.

F. Hurd

Nelson Road

Westward Ho!

North Devon EX39 1LQ

Tel: 01237 474039

Devon clotted cream and homemade sausages.

Loseley Chilled Products

Guildford

Surrey GU3 1HS

Tel: 01483 571881

Cream, yoghurt and cottage cheese.

The Kitchen Garden

Old Down House

Tockington

Bristol BS12 4PG

Tel: 01454 413605

Dairy ice creams and freezer products.

INDEX